# A NATION IN BLOOM

Inspiring everyone to grow

Matthew Biggs

# A NATION IN BLOOM

Celebrating the people, plants and places
of the Royal Horticultural Society

WHITE
LION
PUBLISHING

# Contents

# Foreword

Never has the work of the Royal Horticultural Society been more important or more far reaching. Gone are the days when one of its members addressed a meeting with the words 'No matter how small your garden, always be sure to devote at least four acres to woodland.' The society's membership is no longer the exclusive province of the landed gentry, it is open to anyone who has an interest in gardening and who cares about what we do with our patch of earth, whether that be stately acres, a pocket handkerchief of a back garden or simply a window box on a balcony.

Cultivating plants and beautifying the landscape has been a passion of mine since childhood, and it is a mission that continues to enthral me. But recently I have begun to feel that its importance is dawning on a wider public. Gardening is not simply a matter of enjoying pretty summer bedding plants and hanging baskets, of growing food on allotments and vegetable patches, it is a manifestation of a wider issue – that of conservation and the stewardship of the natural world. Gardeners are not only the custodians of our planet's rich plant life, they are at the cutting edge of ensuring the survival of the world's botanical riches and the environment in which plants grow. This might seem like a rather grandiose claim to make for what to some people is just 'gardening' – brightening our lives with a few roses in the front garden – but it is one in which I firmly believe, and which the Royal Horticultural Society continues to champion.

Today's RHS is hyperactive in its quest to inspire gardeners, to show how important gardening really is and to offer help in the form of education and advice as well as creating a growing number of gardens across Britain where all of us can find solace and stimulation.

These gardens also remind us just how lucky we are to live on a pattern of islands which, thanks to the current climate, is capable of growing a range of plants from sub-arctic flora in the north to Mediterranean natives in the south.

Whatever the future holds regarding climate change, the RHS aims to be on the ball in terms of conserving and sustaining our valuable plant resources, in helping all gardeners to be better at cultivating our rich heritage, and in ensuring, through its Campaign for School Gardening, that those to whom we bequeath our horticultural legacy recognise its importance and enjoy their own custodianship to the full. That's not a bad aim, is it?

*Alan Titchmarsh MBE VMH DL*

# Introduction

Matthew Biggs has written this book at a most relevant and prescient moment in the history of the RHS. It skilfully brings together so much of our past, present and the future. He has brought to life the essence of the learned society and how it has adapted to face the challenges of the day. He does this with the knowledge and skill for which he is renowned.

The RHS has so many different facets but the common theme across all the committees and operations is the importance of people, whether they are staff, volunteers or members. Their knowledge, experience and passion for horticulture is fundamental to the RHS in the wider sense of promoting the benefits in growing plants in all sections of society. Of course, we all see the portraits of the long-bearded botanists of the nineteenth century remind us of their passion for collecting many of the plants which are now common in our gardens. Amid our enthusiasm for the future, we must take care not to let them down.

As the membership base grows so does the RHS ability to reach more people, whether in the UK or abroad. At a time when technology bombards everybody with vast quantities of largely unwanted information, the RHS provides the calm, the theoretical centre of the wheel, where the basic principles of life can be enjoyed and promoted for the benefit of the environment, deprived urban neighbourhoods and those with mental health problems. But the outward-facing part of what we do – the shows, our publishing, community work, science research, beautiful gardens – all reflects the joy of horticulture that we should always promote.

The science that underpins our ability to perform these objectives is being upgraded and the foundations of the learned society being professionally curated. Without an ideological heart organisations can struggle to work out who they are and why they exist. They develop no real mission other than to bolster members for causes that change as the wind of fashion blows from different directions. This is not the RHS. We are steeped in our past, but that is a strength so long as it is used to aid our comprehension of the future.

As we develop and upgrade historic infrastructure, and the physical building work is nearing completion, we can concentrate on the way in which plants and the activity of gardening can provide spiritual fulfilment for those of us who wish to seek respite sometimes from our fast-moving, computer-obsessed generation. Mental health will be a large area of concern for society generally. 'Growing stuff' has been the behaviour of *Homo sapiens* since the earliest of times – we now need to reconnect with that simple activity for the sake of the health of the nation.

The RHS is there to advise those with existing horticultural knowledge, to excite those who want to grow but do not know how to start, and to provide comfort for those who are failed by our society. All this is backed up by science. A learned society which provides a strong sounding board for the future.

*Sir Nicholas Bacon, Bt, RHS President*

The history of the society is as vibrant as the bedding displays seen in RHS gardens in spring and, like the plantings, there is plenty more excitement to come.

Chapter 1
# In pursuit of excellence

# In pursuit of excellence

## THE STORY OF THE RHS

Since its foundation 215 years ago, the RHS has grown from an idea in the mind of a single person to become a large, multifaceted organisation touching the lives of millions of people. Over time the society has survived threats, moved house, reinvented itself, made discoveries, launched careers, and influenced generations of gardeners. It has shaped Britain's gardening and plant heritage and is indisputably part of the nation's cultural landscape. In fact, there is no real equivalent anywhere in the world. The RHS's charitable purpose, which has evolved with the society, is to 'inspire passion and excellence in the science, art and practice of horticulture'. Today it is in many ways entering a new era, by seeking to engage with an even wider audience and make gardening a life-enhancing activity for everyone. The milestone this represents is best measured by looking back at the journey that has led to this point.

It began in the late eighteenth century with John Wedgwood, eldest son of Josiah Wedgwood, the great English potter. When his father died in 1795, John moved to Cote House, near Bristol, to pursue his interests in horticulture and botany, and in 1801 began turning his attention to forming a horticultural society. The idea took root on 7 March 1804, when the Horticultural Society of London was founded in a room above what is now Hatchards bookshop in Piccadilly. Wedgwood was joined by six others: Sir Joseph Banks (left), who had travelled with Captain Cook on the *Endeavour* and was president of the Royal Society; royal gardeners William Forsyth and William Townsend Aiton; Charles Francis Greville, member of parliament and collector of exotic plants; botanist Richard Anthony Salisbury; and nurseryman James Dickson.

Learned societies were a common feature of social life in towns and cities at the time, reflecting a fervent interest in science, art and philosophy. The new horticultural society was formed 'for the improvement of horticulture in all its branches, ornamental as well as useful', to complement the work other societies had done to improve the yield of domestic animals and agriculture. Horticulture, it was felt, had been neglected, and gardeners were routinely carrying out practices inherited from previous generations. By improving techniques and introducing new plant varieties, particularly for wholesome food crops, the society would serve the needs of the country at large. Ornamental plants were included for their value as a source of relaxation and enjoyment, not least in relieving grimy urban living conditions.

By May 1804 the Horticultural Society had enrolled ninety-three fellows (as members were called until 1978). New recruits had to be recommended in writing and personally known to at least three current members. Not surprisingly, the atmosphere was similar to a gentlemen's club. At first they met eight times a year but this extended to the first and third Tuesday of every month. They talked about gardening, exhibited plants and listened to papers, mostly on fruit and vegetables, which from 1807 were published in the society's *Transactions*. Topics included the best varieties of American cranberry, potatoes in hotbeds, overwintering dahlias, and the cultivation techniques adopted in Roman Britain.

If you travelled back to those early years of the society's existence, it might be more familiar than you imagine. Many traits of the current RHS can be traced to those times: a garden, shows, awards, trials and a library. In 1821 the society acquired a house at 21 Regent Street,

[THE GARDENS OF THE HORTICULTURAL SOCIETY AT KENSINGTON GORE.]

London, and leased 13 hectares/33 acres from the Duke of Devonshire's estate in Chiswick (then a riverside village west of the capital) to establish an experimental garden where they would test varieties and cultivation techniques. From 1827 they held floral fetes with competitive classes for flowers and vegetables. Between 1867 and 1873 the society organised annual shows at Bury St Edmunds, Nottingham and other towns (also Cardiff in 1920), forerunners of today's regional shows. The first examinations for gardeners took place in 1836, and plant trials were an important activity by the 1860s. Even the learned discussions have their echoes in the present day, in the work of the RHS specialist plant committees.

The character of the society was greatly influenced by its second president, Thomas Andrew Knight, who held the post from 1811 to 1838. A country gentleman with an affinity for botany and the natural world, he is now recognised as a pioneer of horticultural science for the way he applied scientific principles to practical horticultural problems. He enquired into many subjects, from the design of pineapple pits to the movement of sap in trees, and was an early champion of improving plants through breeding and selection. In mid-century, the society benefitted from the energy of another outstanding horticultural scientist, John Lindley, who served the organisation for over forty years in a number of roles. The society's commitment to research and evidence-based advice, in addition to its contribution to standardising the names of ornamental plants, began in these formative decades.

By the 1820s, when the garden at Chiswick was taking shape, new fellows were required to pay 5 guineas on joining and then an annual subscription of 3 guineas. This was a considerable sum – equivalent to around £2,500–£4,000 in purchasing power today – and fellows inevitably came from the wealthier social classes. However, the society allowed professional gardeners a special class of membership if they had received a medal or had a paper printed in the *Transactions*. There were also honorary fellows (royalty, on the whole) and corresponding fellows who lived abroad and were expected to send interesting plant material or information to the society.

The owners of country estates, some of them sponsors of the great plant hunters, competed at RHS shows with rare and unusual plants like orchids, magnolias and camellias. The Veitch Memorial Medal, instituted in 1870, commemorated James Veitch of Chelsea, whose nursery, one of the greatest of its era, introduced thousands of new garden and conservatory plants into cultivation from around the globe. From 1830 a small number of female fellows were admitted, including Louisa Lawrence, a prolific and award-winning exhibitor of plants, who was also first to coax the tropical tree *Amherstia nobilis* into flower. Fellows living far from London were less able to visit the society's garden and shows, so in 1894 a bye-law was passed giving those over 56 kilometres/35 miles away double the share of seeds and plants that were distributed from Chiswick each year.

The financial fortunes of the society fluctuated over the first fifty years, reaching their lowest point in 1858–9, when the lack of income from membership and the fall in proceeds from its Chiswick garden precipitated the sale of 21 Regent Street and its library containing many rare books and original drawings. (The herbarium had been sacrificed in 1856.) The society only survived through the determination of several influential members and the support of Prince Albert, elected president in 1858. He arranged for the society

HIS ROYAL HIGHNESS,
FREDERICK WILLIAM, PRINCE ROYAL OF PRUSSIA

Left: The second RHS garden in Kensington was grand and formal, reflecting the style of its era.

Above: Beautiful, ornate and full of flowers, this document containing the signature of Prince Frederick William (1795–1861) is part of the RHS Lindley Library's unique collection of royal signatures. It was made to commemorate royal patrons and fellows of the RHS on 19 April 1825.

Above, right: The RHS owe a debt of gratitude to Thomas Andrew Knight (1758–1838), whose ideas and industry were the foundation of the society we know today.

Right: John Wedgwood worked for the family pottery company and as a banker in London. It was he who proposed creating a new horticultural society to Joseph Banks and the other founder members.

Above: A rose show at the Horticultural Society's gardens in Kensington, taken from the *Illustrated London News*, 12 July 1873. The dress code, clearly, is very different to today.

Below: The Rock Garden was one of the first features to be created after Wisley was given to the RHS. It is a marked contrast to the current example, in both planting and style.

Right, above: The RHS New Hall (now the Lindley Hall) was opened by King Edward VII, and the guests were addressed by Sir Trevor Lawrence, then president of the society.

Right: The balcony of the Lawrence Hall during an exhibition has been the perfect place for people watching and an overview of the fabulous nursery displays since the 1920s.

Supplement to *Amateur Gardening*, May 23rd, 1914.

THE ROCK GARDEN AT WISLEY IN MAY.

Drawing prepared for Amateur Gardening.            Printed by W. H. & L. Collingridge, London    [Copyright.]

to be renamed the Royal Horticultural Society and ensured that it had a new garden in Kensington, where shows could be held nearer the centre of London. In 1862 the first Great Spring Show was held here, the earliest incarnation of the Chelsea Flower Show. Queen Victoria, the society's royal patron since the beginning of her reign, busied herself in the 1860s with recruiting as large a royal membership for the society as she could, including the entire French royal family in exile. (The RHS created the Victoria Medal of Honour on the occasion of her diamond jubilee in 1897, an accolade held by only sixty-three eminent horticulturists at one time, corresponding to the number of years in her reign.)

Membership revived in the second half of the nineteenth century and revenues increased. In 1866 the society was able to purchase John Lindley's book collection, which has gradually developed into one of the world's finest horticultural libraries. With the approach of its centenary year, the society sought another permanent home and secured a 999-year lease on offices and an exhibition hall at 80 Vincent Square, in central London. On 22 July 1904, the Lindley Hall (as it has been known since its refurbishment in 2000) was opened by Edward VII, the first of the fortnightly London flower shows being held there just four days later. The society's headquarters and the London branch of the Lindley Library have been located at Vincent Square ever since.

As declared by a newspaper advert in 1900, the RHS was also searching for a new garden 'beyond the radius of the London smoke'. The solution arrived in 1903, when the society received in trust, as a gift from Sir Thomas Hanbury, 24 hectares/60 acres of freehold land at Wisley, in Surrey, previously the garden of former council member G.F. Wilson. (The Chiswick site was abandoned at this point and built

over; the Kensington garden had ceased in 1888.) The Hanbury Trust stipulated that the society use the Wisley estate as an experimental garden for the 'encouragement and improvement of scientific and practical horticulture in all its branches'. To this end, a small laboratory was opened, the School of Horticulture was founded to prepare students for the career of professional gardener, and the trials of flowers, fruit and vegetables were resumed. Wisley received 6,000 visits in the first year. One of the first ornamental additions was a rock garden.

The acquisition of Wisley was a pivotal moment, offering security and the chance to expand. In 1913 the Great Spring Show transferred to the grounds of the Royal Hospital at Chelsea, where it has remained. The first Award of Garden Merit – in those days made on the recommendation of the Wisley Garden Committee – was given in 1922 to *Hamamelis mollis* (witch hazel) as a plant of outstanding excellence for garden use. The fortnightly flower shows held in Lindley Hall were becoming more popular, to the point that exhibitors and visitors complained of overcrowding. So the RHS decided to lease land nearby and build New Hall (now Lawrence Hall), which opened in 1928. In another expansionary move, the RHS Council decided to open Wisley on Sundays.

Membership started to grow more rapidly in the first half of the twentieth century. Between 1900 and 1939 the number of fellows rose from 5,000 to around 30,000, climbing again to 50,000 by 1956. During the Second World War the RHS had published *The Vegetable Garden Displayed*, in support of the government's Dig for Victory campaign. It took a definite step into book publishing in 1951 with the *Dictionary of Gardening*, a monumental work in four volumes. A more commercial outlook was signalled with the foundation of RHS

Left: The angles in the elegant architecture of the Laboratory are reflected in the terraced landscape and the Jellicoe Canal. Note the impressive chimneys.

Left, below: A lavender wisteria brings class and style to the frontage of Rosemoor House, once the home of Lady Anne Palmer, who gifted her garden and land to the RHS.

The story continues......
William Lobb (1809 – 1864) was employed by Veitch Nurseries of Exeter to collect new plants from across the world. During his travels he sent back herbarium specimens and live plants, as well as huge quantities of seed. These were propagated, grown and offered for sale by Veitch. The methods used to propagate these plants in the twenty-first century have changed little from James Veitch's day but the facilities and equipment have; our propagation fact sheets detail these changes.

In its heyday the Veitch Nursery would have used the same basic propagation methods and techniques that modern nurserymen use today: seed, cuttings, division, layers and grafting. Plants were grown on in the field, and plants difficult to transplant were grown in pots. It is only the facilities and equipment that have changed. The display shows some of the ways in which plants were propagated and grown at Exeter, and later at the Chelsea nurseries.

'The deeper financial crisis of 2009 was met with restructuring and the redundancy of eighty gardeners. It was a difficult time from which the RHS emerged ready to start building again on the achievements of the past.'

Left, top: Workmen begin creating a rock garden, in front of the supporting pillars for the marquee, during the build up to Chelsea in 1936.

Left, bottom: Botanist and plantsman Chris Brickell CBE, VMH, was appointed the first director general in 1985.

Above: The RHS supports and promotes other gardening charities. This display by Pershore College in the Plant Heritage Marquee at Hampton Court Palace Flower Show in 2009 showed propagation techniques that had been in use 200 years before.

Enterprises Ltd in 1975, starting with the sale of gifts and books, then plants. In the same year, the RHS journal was renamed *The Garden* to reflect a more populist approach. Another change of gear came in 1985, when plantsman and botanist Chris Brickell was appointed as the RHS's first director general, and by the 1990s the society had become a mass membership organisation.

Recent decades have brought more gardens and new flower shows. Rosemoor, in Devon, was presented to the society in 1987 by Lady Anne Palmer. The RHS inherited Hyde Hall, Essex, in 1993, then merged with the Northern Horticultural Society in 2001, taking over their garden at Harlow Carr, near Harrogate. The RHS also formed partnerships with other organisations, regional colleges and gardens, offering a wide range of events and visits to gardeners.

While the society had already weathered several post-war recessions, the deeper financial crisis of 2009 was met with restructuring and the redundancy of eighty gardeners. It was a difficult time from which the RHS emerged ready to start building again on the achievements of the past. Exactly where it is heading is explored in the next chapter. It is clear that Thomas Andrew Knight's desire for the society to 'exceed the hopes of its founders' has most certainly been fulfilled.

The Rose Garden at Hyde Hall attracts visitors with beauty and fragrance and the bonus of a wonderful view down to the glasshouse in the Global Growth Vegetable Garden and out into the landscape beyond.

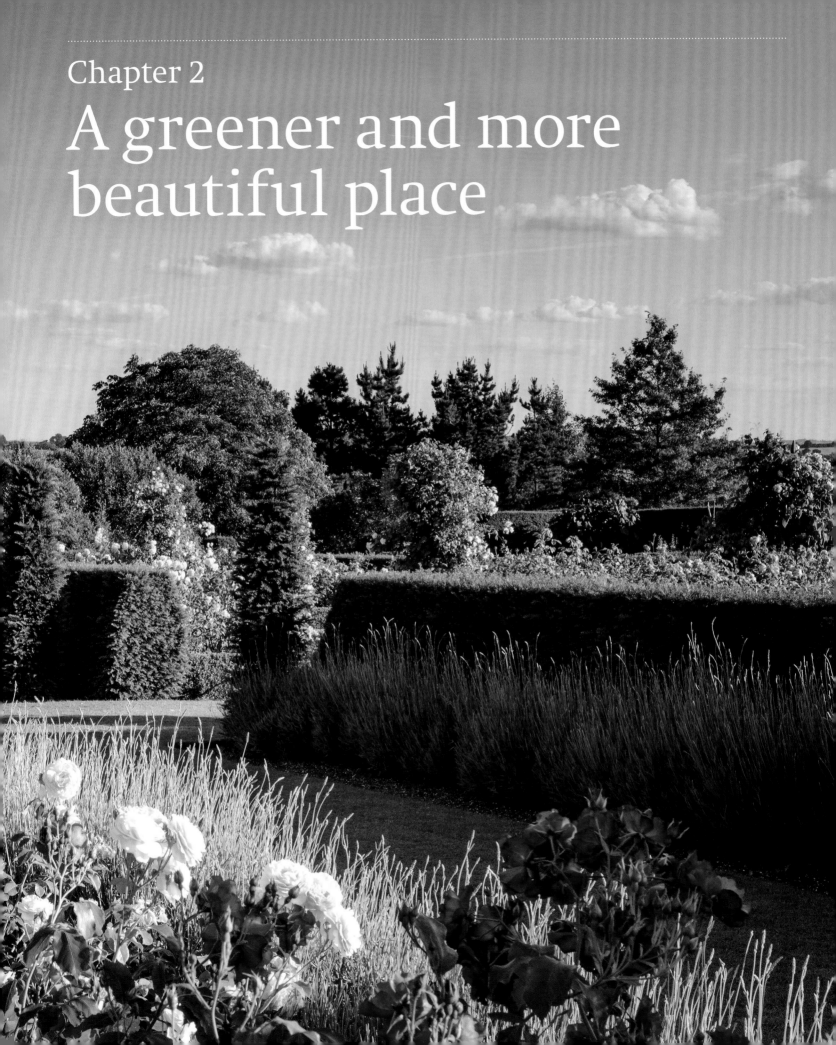

# Chapter 2
# A greener and more beautiful place

Left: 'The South West Water Green Garden', designed by Tom Simpson for the 2018 RHS Hampton Court Palace Flower Show, explored sustainable rainwater management and showed off plants in all their verdant glory.

Right: *Verbascum* and *Echinops* energise the Mixed Borders at RHS Garden Wisley, with a boost of bright yellow and blue.

# A greener and more beautiful place

## INVESTING IN THE FUTURE OF HORTICULTURE

Energy levels are high at the RHS these days. Things are moving on. There is a stronger sense of purpose, greater cohesion across its activities, and an undeniable note of excitement about the future. These are also signs of a deeper change, brought about as the RHS shifts decisively from being a traditional learned society to becoming a dynamic, forward-thinking and inclusive charity relevant to the needs of all gardeners in the twenty-first century. The society has found its focus, and all the work it does is coalescing around this more compelling message.

The RHS vision is to enrich everyone's life through plants, and make the UK a greener and more beautiful place. This statement appears on the front cover of a document laying out what the RHS wants to achieve by 2025. It's a big ambition – but why has it emerged now? It certainly wasn't provoked by a crisis. The society was in a comfortable position as an organisation at the turn of the millennium, with around a quarter of a million members (it now has half a million), and was already sharing its passion for plants through its gardens, shows and publications. There was, however, a risk of stagnation, and the arrival of a new director general, Sue Biggs, in 2010 was the right time to ask questions about the society's future direction. 'We decided to put science at the heart of everything we do,' says Sue, 'and to join this up with what people want to find out about for their gardens.' Couple that with a growing environmental and wildlife awareness, plus the immense benefit of plants and gardens to people (especially across different communities), and the strategic direction was becoming refined. This brought into perspective why the RHS matters as a charity and how it makes a greater difference to society and the environment by engaging with more people through community initiatives.

Over the next decade the RHS will see through a challenging £160-million investment programme that will allow it to share the benefits of gardening more widely. This is being funded from member and supporter donations, an improved financial performance year-on-year, and by realising the value of former investments. Most notable was the 999-year lease of the Lawrence Hall in London to Westminster School, which released £18 million for future projects. External funding of £40 million was also needed, of which more than half has already been secured. It is a massive task, considering that the largest sum the RHS had ever raised before was £7 million for the Wisley Glasshouse.

The investment programme focuses on seven key projects, designed to set the society's gardens, outward work and collections in good order for the next generation – but also to push the organisation forward. As Sue explains, this is about much more than buildings and infrastructure: 'it's what goes on in those buildings that counts, what happens as a result of our staff at our sites, and the way we engage much more broadly with all types of gardeners.' Getting the message of the RHS out to different people, different communities and different interests is at the centre of this ambitious project.

Four of the investment projects are happening at RHS gardens, including the creation of a magnificent new garden to serve the north-west of Britain (RHS Garden Bridgewater in Salford, Greater Manchester), and a fifth project has upgraded and improved the Lindley Library in London. The other two will boost the RHS's charitable work for the Horticulture Matters campaign (raising

the status of horticulture as a career), and allow it to extend its commitment to community outreach and urban gardens. Some of the projects began in 2015 and results can already be seen – such as substantial changes at Hyde Hall, in Essex – but many exciting developments are yet to come. Major transformations are in store for Wisley, including the construction of a National Centre for Horticultural Science and Learning.

Across the four garden projects, common elements emerge: welcoming a broader range of visitors, excellence in horticulture, creating a distinct identity, and ensuring year-round interest. New garden features will revolve around key themes such as growing food, plants for pollinators, gardening for wellbeing and adapting to a changing climate. There will be fresh inspiration, lots of ideas to try at home and examples of how we can garden more responsibly. The RHS gardens will continue to function as living laboratories, demonstrating new practical techniques and planting styles, probing scientific questions, assessing the performance of garden plants and testing how they tolerate environmental stresses such as drought and cold. Knowledge gained in this way will be shared with millions of visitors and the wider gardening community.

What is particularly encouraging is how the RHS is currently opening up and sharing more of what it does. Some of its work will come out from behind the scenes for the first time, as visitors to Wisley's forthcoming science centre will have views into the herbarium, laboratories and seed department. Likewise, a new exhibition space at the Lindley Library allows rare and beautiful works to come out of storage and be shown to the public. In its role as a global knowledge bank, the RHS is digitising its library and

herbarium collections so they can be made available online, and it will be providing greater access to advice through its shows, gardens and website.

Traditionally, gardening was something you took up when you bought your first house; and in the past, the RHS has perhaps reinforced the notion that a 'true' gardener was someone who raises plants from seed and knows how to prune roses. Today, the vision is much wider, so that Britain's 27 million gardeners as well as all the RHS members can benefit from the increased impact of the society's work. Believing that everyone, everywhere deserves contact with plants, the RHS also wants to engage with people who have little or no growing space of their own, or who have never gardened before.

Learning at all levels is – and needs to be – a priority. This can be seen in the shape of new education centres and teaching gardens, which will provide more opportunities for children to connect with nature at RHS gardens and learn vital life skills. Young people and adults will be supported to learn new skills, particularly beginner gardeners. The RHS is also helping to train the next generation of horticulturists and horticultural scientists, and is providing more places for students and apprentices in its gardens.

Community gardening is known to have positive effects on social cohesion, health and wellbeing, employability and ecosystem services. Through its investment programme the RHS will be expanding its work with community groups, especially in urban areas. Each RHS garden will also be strengthening links with local communities, and there will continue to be community involvement at flower shows. Volunteers already make an enormous contribution to enhancing local areas through Britain in Bloom and related RHS

Left: A 3D model of the National Centre for Horticultural Science and Learning at RHS Garden Wisley provided inspiration and momentum at the start of the Strategic Investment Project.

Above: TV presenter Frances Tophill and pupils of Hammersmith Academy, winners of the RHS School Gardening Team of the Year 2017, enjoy their time gardening together.

Right: Play consultation events at RHS Garden Wisley ensure that learning about plants and gardening is always absorbing, fascinating and fun.

Below: Scientists in the Laboratory at Wisley use analytical equipment with a level of sophistication that their predecessors would never have imagined.

campaigns such as It's Your Neighbourhood and Greening Grey Britain. The huge potential that volunteers represent has recently been demonstrated at the RHS's new garden, Bridgewater, where hundreds of people have come forward to help. The RHS wants to do more to support and value volunteers throughout the organisation and in villages, towns and cities across the UK.

The RHS is the only place in the world where scientific research is dedicated to the challenges faced by gardeners, and this position will be strengthened in coming years. The new science centre, housing three state-of-the-art laboratories for diagnostics, molecular and environmental research, will establish the RHS at the forefront of horticultural science. Work will continue to focus on problems such as pests and diseases, preparing for the effects of climate change and the correct naming of garden plants. The results will be used by the horticultural industry, government and policymakers, and help millions of gardeners through RHS campaigns, its publishing and the advisory service. By investing in science, and building on its extensive connections and partnerships with other organisations, the RHS can become an increasing influence in world horticulture. We may see it becoming more vocal on issues of concern in the future.

The RHS is determined to make a difference. In the future, we will see more children discovering the health and wellbeing benefits of gardens, more young people choosing careers in horticulture, more residents with access to beautifully planted public places, and hundreds of thousands more people inspired to grow plants in their gardens and outdoor spaces. We will see more high-quality advice and information shared with people in the UK and around the world, more scientific research that helps gardeners make informed choices, greater knowledge of the cultivated-plant diversity in the UK and an increased appreciation of the UK's 500 years of gardening heritage.

Of course, none of this could be achieved without the invaluable support of the new half-million RHS members. They are at the core of the work the charity undertakes, but a balance is needed to ensure there is plenty for members to be proud of while welcoming in other visitors and engaging different audiences. From shows to publications, science to trials, gardens to community outreach, there is a multitude of ways the RHS can help to benefit people, plants and the planet. And with the current verve and excitement across the society, this all looks set to grow.

> 'The RHS is determined to make a difference. In the future, we will see more children discovering the health and wellbeing benefits of gardens.'

Left, top: Wisley community allotmenteers on their plots, standing by and ready for action.

Left, bottom: The 'Taking Stock Garden' on the Sheerwater Estate, Woking, was designed by RHS student Nick Keenan and created by the Community Outreach Team, the School of Horticulture, local residents and Woking Council: one of many successful collaborations undertaken by RHS community outreach.

Above: The plant centres in the RHS gardens are filled with tempting plants and garden accessories all displayed perfectly, so it is not easy to resist.

Right: The RHS flag flies proudly over the entrance to the RHS offices in Vincent Square, London. This is the main administrative centre for the society. Within this building, staff organise shows, manage archives, speak to members and work to make sure that the RHS remains a positive and creative driving force for gardening in the twenty-first century.

## RHS GARDEN WISLEY, SURREY

There are major developments ahead for the RHS's flagship garden. The centrepiece of the project, the National Centre for Horticultural Science and Learning (due to open in 2020), will hold three new laboratories for collaborative research, a more spacious herbarium adapted to preserving this important collection of pressed plants, an advisory hub, learning studios and an inspirational public atrium. Located at Hilltop, the Y-shaped building will be surrounded by three educational gardens: the World Food Garden and Wildlife Garden, designed by Ann-Marie Powell, and the Wellbeing Garden, designed by Matt Keightley. At Wisley's main garden entrance, an avenue of 90 cherry trees set in a landscape designed by Christopher Bradley-Hole will take visitors to the new Welcome Building, with cafe, restaurant, shop and extensive plant centre, from where they will step into Seven Acres. The iconic Grade II-listed Arts and Crafts-style Laboratory will be enhanced by the removal of modern buildings, and be open to the public as a museum and exhibition space.

Above: A drone's eye view as building work progressed at Wisley. As new buildings appeared, visitors watched developments from a viewpoint in the car park, which became very popular as a result.

Below: This was a first glimpse of the entrance of the new Welcome Building as it was in October 2018.

Right, top: An architect's visualisation of the Wisley Hilltop building reveals the elegant curves of the new gardens surrounding the science centre, and offers a tantalising glimpse of the future.

Right, bottom: The new National Centre for Horticultural Science and Learning, as imagined by an architect showed it to be an elegant, slender, contemporary building. WilkinsonEyre, the architects behind the design, are famous for their futuristic work at the Gardens by the Bay in Singapore.

## RHS GARDEN BRIDGEWATER, SALFORD, GREATER MANCHESTER

Opening in 2020, the RHS's fifth garden will bring a wealth of beautiful plants and gardening expertise to the north-west of England. This far-reaching project will initially focus on the huge Walled Garden, as the setting for new community teaching plots, a Kitchen Garden designed by Charlotte Harris and Hugo Bugg, and a Paradise Garden designed by Tom Stuart-Smith. Strong links with the local community will be at the heart of Bridgewater, which will also pay tribute to the area's fascinating history. It is hoped the garden can contribute to the health and wellbeing of people living in urban areas nearby, inspire people to garden in new and more conscientious ways, and make horticultural education accessible to thousands of children. The garden will host a full calendar of events, including shows, and provide an on-site advice service and library. Further phases of development will bring more exciting features to Bridgewater in coming years.

Below: Construction works at RHS Garden Bridgewater involved the dispersal of vast volumes of earth around the site.

Bottom: Tom Stuart-Smith's ambitious masterplan for the entire RHS Bridgewater site.

Right, top: The imposing angular architecture of Hyde Hall Learning Centre and restaurant creates a sharp contrast to the billowing form of the Dry Garden and the fluffy clouds above.

Right, bottom: After inspiring people to garden, visitor centres at RHS gardens offer all that is needed to get gardening – and more, from plants to tools and RHS publications.

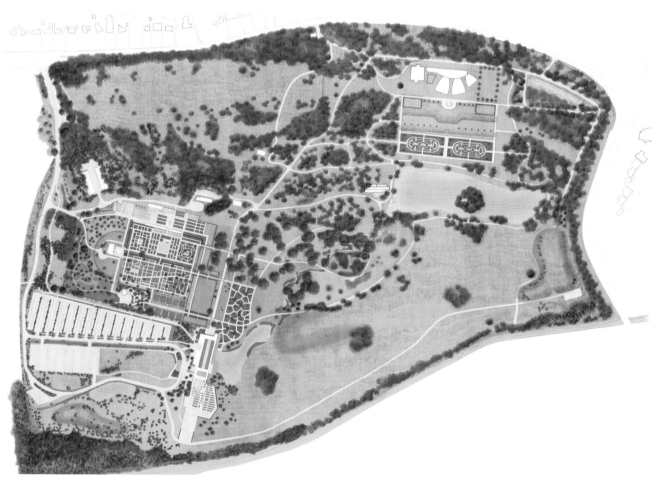

### RHS GARDEN HYDE HALL, ESSEX

Horticultural inspiration is at the heart of improvements at Hyde Hall, many of them completed in 2018 in keeping with landscape designer Adam Frost's hilltop masterplan. Priorities here have been to increase biodiversity by planting trees and meadows, to lead the way in water management and sustainable gardening, and to expand Hyde Hall's schools' programme so thousands more children can benefit. The new Global Growth Vegetable Garden, designed by Xa Tollemache, promotes healthy eating and the pleasures of fresh food, while the Winter Garden gives Hyde Hall further seasonal interest. Planting for the UK's largest perennial meadow has begun; this will be a food source for birds, bees and butterflies, and links the garden to the wider landscape. It will also hopefully be the starting point for smaller meadows in gardens and communities. Beautiful new buildings, designed by Cullinan Studio, include the Clore Learning Centre and teaching garden, an improved Visitor Centre for a warmer welcome, and a new Hilltop activities centre and restaurant.

## COMMUNITY OUTREACH AND URBAN GARDENS

The RHS will build on its community outreach work by increasing the opportunities for people living in cities to get involved in gardening and enjoy beautiful green spaces. It will support a number of urban gardens across Britain by providing financial aid and horticultural advice, so that as many people as possible can get involved. Each garden will be shaped by the communities living locally who put time into caring for and shaping them. These will be places where people can reconnect with nature, grow fresh food and improve their overall sense of wellbeing. They will also be social spaces, enabling diverse groups and people of all ages to meet up, garden together and exchange ideas on how we can live more sustainably. By focusing on communities – in some ways, the real legacy of the investment programme – the RHS will bring the benefits of plants to a wider audience and ultimately transform lives.

Below: One RHS outreach project worked with the charity Young Saheliya in Glasgow to green the grey courtyard at their centre. The project helps women and girls from a range of minority-ethnic backgrounds to gain skills, find new friends, learn the English language and boost their self-esteem. Gardening really does change lives.

Below: The Streamside Garden, running the length of Harlow Carr – one of the longest of its kind in the country – is home to a vibrant display of colourful, moisture-loving plants. The gardeners have selected their own special strain of primulas in a kaleidoscope of pink, peach, orange, yellow and purple, known as the Harlow Carr hybrids.

## RHS GARDEN HARLOW CARR, NORTH YORKSHIRE

Developments are well underway at Harlow Carr, improving the quality of horticulture throughout, enhancing the garden's distinct identity and strengthening ties with the local community. The woodland has been opened up and enlivened with spring bulbs, and the much-loved Streamside replanted with spectacular blue Himalayan poppies (*Meconopsis*) and primulas. A new feature on the theme of small gardens will give visitors more ideas to try at home. Most significantly for Harlow Carr's future, the RHS has purchased the neighbouring Harrogate Arms, reuniting the garden with the building that was Harrogate's first 'bath house' and thereby restoring its historic context. Once work to the house is complete (incorporating a new exhibition space), a tailor-made garden will be created around it.

Below: Staff in the Lindley Library ensure that as many publications as possible are on display: a subtle reminder to visitors of the wealth and diversity of material held in the library and archives, and a way of introducing students to new perspectives on their work.

## RHS LINDLEY LIBRARY, LONDON

The exceptional collections of books, art, photographs, nursery catalogues and ephemera at the RHS Lindley Library are a reflection of the UK's rich gardening heritage, but in the past access to this store of knowledge has been limited. An extensive programme of digitisation will eventually make documents freely available online, opening them up to researchers, art lovers and the general public around the world. The building at Vincent Square was refurbished in 2016, providing an enhanced Upper Reading Room (which is an open-access lending library), improved storage conditions to safeguard RHS heritage collections for future generations, and a new exhibition space with facilities to display rarely seen archive elements. The inaugural exhibition revealed beautiful illustrations from early Japanese nursery catalogues.

Below: Staff in the Lindley Library ensure that as many publications as possible are on display: a subtle reminder to visitors of the wealth and diversity of material held in the library and archives, and a way of introducing students to new perspectives on their work.

## HORTICULTURE MATTERS

Through this ongoing campaign, the RHS works with others in the sector to raise the profile of the horticultural industry and address Britain's looming shortage in skilled horticulturists. The aim is to bring about a wholesale shift in awareness for a generation of children and young adults to come. By changing perceptions in schools, the RHS hopes to make more students aware of the attractive and rewarding careers that horticulture offers. The society also keeps the government informed about the value of horticulture to the UK's economy, health and environment. In its own gardens, more places have been made available for students and apprentices; and the commitment to school gardening and investment in postgraduate research will continue to expand.

Below: One of the advantages of being an RHS student is the opportunity to gain experience in all the departments in the garden. While planting up the subtropical border they can learn Latin names, discover which are their favourites, place them correctly and practise planting techniques. Gardeners never stop learning.

Gardens change according to the weather and light. This view from the Rock Garden as the sun sets in spring is a perfect example.

Left, clockwise from top left: The Jubilee Arboretum bursts into life with the green shoots of spring; Oakwood is illuminated with the autumn colour of *Acer palmatum* 'Elegans'; blue *Camassia leichtlinii* subsp. *suksdorfii* Caerulea Group in the foreground with the roof of the Laboratory just showing beyond; members of the Dahlia Sub-committee on the Trials Field – 'all in favour, raise your hand'; the Walled Garden in spring is full of strong architectural shapes; (left) until recently, this venerable *Prunus* 'Shirotae' underplanted with *Muscari armeniacum* lit up Seven Acres in spring, but (right) *Prunus* 'Matsumae-kofuku' and *Erythronium* 'Pagoda' still brighten the margins of the Rock Garden; the Laboratory, for decades the focus of scientific research for the benefit of gardeners, will be transformed into a visitor attraction.

Right: Wisley has always been a working garden, a haven for horticultural knowledge and experiment. This aerial view in the 1950s shows series ranks of glasshouses and beds. Quite a bit has changed since then, but the ethos of plants and plantsmanship haven't.

# Wisley

## SURREY GARDEN

The oldest and most revered of the RHS gardens is a lively place in all seasons. Its wide-ranging appeal to families, schoolchildren, gardening clubs, horticultural students and day trippers places it among the UK's top visitor attractions and makes it one of the country's best-loved gardens. Many people come to enjoy the colours, scents and open spaces, drawn by the RHS's reputation for horticultural excellence. For others, Wisley is a workplace and the home of RHS science. The experience of all concerned will be enhanced by exciting developments on the horizon. As the strategic investment project unfolds, new landscapes and gardens will take their place among Wisley's iconic and cherished features.

Over time, Wisley has amassed all the elements expected of an influential garden, covering every aspect of horticulture, from lawns and trees to alpine and tropical glasshouses, and the growing of fruit, vegetables and herbs. becoming the garden that is so familiar today. It is world-famous for growing a wide range of plants to the highest standards, and many of the numerous collections are historic and of national significance. The collection of rhododendrons, for example, includes more than 1,000 accessions, of which 500 are rare or endangered in cultivation. Around the garden visitors will also find 300 kinds of camellia, over 200 magnolias, 730 different apple trees, as well as many Champion Trees – the largest of their kind in the British Isles.

The original site at Wisley was purchased by George Fergusson Wilson in 1878, a keen gardener and a former treasurer of the RHS. His aim was to create the 'Oakwood experimental garden', which rapidly gained a reputation for its collections of gentians, Japanese irises, lilies, primulas and aquatic plants. After his death, it came into the possession of the RHS in 1903 when Sir Thomas Hanbury bought the garden and neighbouring Glebe Farm, and presented the whole 24 hectares/60 acres to the RHS. Since then, the site has been hugely expanded: there are now 70 hectares/172 acres of garden set in 135 hectares/334 acres of land.

One of the first major projects, in 1905, was the construction of a range of glasshouses on what is now the Jellicoe Canal, followed by the Rock Garden, when a light railway had to be installed from the main road to move in the huge Sussex sandstone blocks. These are positioned in the same orientation they had when quarried, creating a natural landscape.

As the garden developed, and the number of staff and students increased, additional facilities for research and training were needed. A local firm was commissioned to build a new Laboratory, which was completed in 1916. Designed to look as if it pre-dated the garden, it was built with materials recycled from old manor houses. Today it is an iconic building that all visitors pass by and remark upon on their way into the garden.

Facing the Laboratory is the Water Lily Pavilion, which was once the humble potting shed; beyond that are the Walled Gardens east and west. One contains an attractive parterre trialling a range of alternatives to traditional box (*Buxus*) hedges; the other is a foliage garden, with many new varieties of *Hosta* and several large Chinese windmill palms (*Trachycarpus fortunei*).

Previously known as the Wild Garden, Oakwood is home to the most diverse plant collection in the garden. The moist, fertile

soil and light shade are ideal for choice herbaceous and bulbous woodland plants, including hostas, primulas and trilliums. Camellias, rhododendrons and magnolias provide colour in spring, followed in early summer by candelabra primulas, foxgloves, stately giant Himalayan lily (*Cardiocrinum giganteum*), and soft pink-flowered *Rosa* 'Paul's Himalayan Musk', which grows high into the canopy of trees. Opposite the neighbouring Rock Garden, giant rhubarb (*Gunnera manicata*) dominates the edge of Oakwood, and planted alongside it, by way of contrast, is its diminutive relative *Gunnera magellanica*, barely 5 centimetres/2 inches tall. Come late autumn and early winter, the first camellias begin to bloom. White-flowered, fragrant *Camellia sasanqua* 'Alba' scents the air in November and December, followed in late winter by the vivid, spidery flowers of witch hazel (*Hamamelis*).

Wisley's famous double borders frame the broad, grassy slope leading to Battleston Hill. They are impressively long and filled with bold colour and texture from late spring right until autumn, peaking from mid- to late summer. Permanent shrubs and trees in the planting include the foxglove tree (*Paulownia tomentosa*), golden Indian bean tree (*Catalpa bignonioides* 'Aurea'), red-barked dogwood (*Cornus alba* 'Elegantissima'), and selected varieties of butterfly bush (*Buddleja davidii*).

The border is graded from cool pastels to hot colours in the centre, then back to cool again. At the cooler ends sit perennials with silvery leaves and white, blue and purple flowers, and in the hot section visitors will find flowers ranging from cerise-pink to bright red and golden yellow, as well as deeply coloured foliage. In late summer and autumn, the feathery delicacy of grass seed heads combine with dahlias, sedums, salvias and monkshoods.

A new wisteria walk links the old garden entrance to the Mixed Borders. In time it will become a glorious purple tunnel of racemes each May, complementing Wisley's already impressive portfolio of wisteria. It is planted with two selections of *Wisteria floribunda*: dark 'Royal Purple' and light mauve 'Kimono'. To give year-round interest and a sense of fun, twenty distinctive pieces of topiary are planted either side of the walk.

The far end of the Mixed Borders rises up on to Battleston Hill. Beyond here lies a beautiful woodland garden, at its peak in late spring, when masses of camellias, magnolias, rhododendrons and azaleas, which thrive on Wisley's acid soil, burst into bloom. Winding footpaths lead visitors past many fine and mature trees, notably Chinese cedar (*Toona sinensis* 'Flamingo'), named for its bright salmon-pink spring foliage. A stumpery in a dell is an unexpected pleasure, with its ferns, Wollemi pines, palms, tree ferns – and a wooden dinosaur hidden among the foliage.

Mediterranean terraces sit on the south side of Battleston Hill, one of the few areas of the garden laid out in geographical order. First created in 1990 and replanted in 2012, this is where plants from Chile, New Zealand, Australia and South Africa flourish in the extra sunshine and free-draining, sandy soil. Eucalyptus, winter-flowering acacias, and cold-tolerant cacti and succulents create a distinctly exotic feel. Many of the trees and shrubs here contain high levels of aromatic oils, which perfume the air on hot days.

The terraces are a wonderful viewpoint for the Trials Field below. Covering several acres, here plants are grown and assessed for garden-worthiness, and the best will be given the RHS Award of Garden Merit (AGM, see pages 202–5). Flowering trials can be spectacular *en masse*

and in spring and summer there are many fascinating displays, including edible plants.

Created and opened in 2017, on the site of what was once a garden devoted to hybrid tea roses, the Exotic Garden showcases plants with a tropical vibe that will flourish outdoors in a typical British summer. It is best described as a formal garden with informal planting – filled with large-leaved plants and vibrant flowers. Palms jostle with hardy bananas for leaf space, and cannas, gingers and dahlias add splashes of colour. Many of these plants are not reliably winter hardy, so they must be wrapped for frost protection, creating a surreal and almost alien scene when visitors pass through in winter.

Constructed in 1910–12, the Rock Garden is among Wisley's oldest and most magnificent features, planted with large groups of alpine plants. This steep, north-facing slope suits plants preferring a cool, shady aspect, while sun-loving plants grow happily on the more exposed outcrops. Numerous small paths weave around the rocks and pools, linked by streams and cascades, with a dramatic waterfall and Japanese landscape on the upper section. The water eventually finds its way to the long ponds below, where a rustic bridge is draped with lilac-blue *Wisteria floribunda* f. *multijuga* in spring. Yellow flags (*Iris pseudacorus*) and Asian candelabra primulas thrive in the moist soil nearby.

Sitting alongside is the grassy slope of an alpine meadow, famous for its carpets of spring and autumn bulbs. First to flower is a large collection of snowdrops on the uppermost ridges, followed in early spring by a carpet of blue as the first crocuses, *Crocus tommasinianus* and *Crocus vernus*, bloom, transforming the area

'A garden that once seemed impervious to change is now on the move. The investment project will revitalise Wisley, offering visitors even more to see and do.'

The Rock Garden on a frosty morning, filled with perfectly poised plants, is a study in balance, structure and form in every season.

completely. The meadow is at its peak in mid-spring when dotted with thousands of sulphur-yellow hoop petticoat daffodils (*Narcissus bulbocodium*). Swathes of dog's-tooth violets (*Erythronium dens-canis*), snake's-head fritillaries (*Fritillaria meleagris*) and anemones follow in late spring, giving way in early summer to spikes of *Dactylorhiza* orchids. Once the bulbs cease flowering, the grass remains uncut so plants can self-seed and butterflies and other insects take food and shelter. The meadow is closely mown in late summer before autumn-flowering crocuses (*Crocus speciosus*) emerge.

Above the Rock Garden are two large alpine houses, displaying varieties of alpine plant from around the world. The Alpine Display House is planted in a formal, Victorian style, and here plants are grown in small pots, sunk into sand-filled benches and replaced regularly to ensure the display is always at its peak. The Landscape Alpine House, on the other hand, replicates natural alpine habitats. It holds a permanent display of alpines planted in a dry gully between 1.5 metre-/5 foot-high 'cliffs', the perfect spot for plants that are difficult to cultivate. Outside are drystone walls, sinks, troughs and a Crevice Garden, all planted with alpines that can be grown outdoors in a limited space.

The RHS has always maintained an outstanding fruit collection. As well as more than 700 apple cultivars, grouped into dessert and culinary types arranged according to their season of ripening, the orchard is home to 175 pear and 100 plum selections. Many other types of fruit are represented, including collections of cider apples and cultivars with good disease resistance. There are also fruit trees on dwarfing rootstocks, and the fruit demonstration area shows how these trees can be grown in restricted, ornamental forms such as step-overs, espaliers, cordons and pyramids – all perfect for the smaller home

garden. Some of the fruit is sold to the public at the visitor entrance – an excellent opportunity to try interesting and different tastes.

A small landscaped hill known as the Viewing Mount, where new plantings of rosemary and lavender will create a striking effect, gives superb views over the orchard and the scenery beyond. Nearby, visitors will encounter displays of strawberries, rhubarb, figs and other soft fruits, including the National Plant Collection of red and white currants. A small vineyard was planted in 2004 to demonstrate viticulture in the British climate using the white wine grapes 'Phönix' and 'Orion'. It yields a small volume of Wisley wine every year.

Wisley's beautifully kept and popular Vegetable Garden shows how edibles and ornamentals can work well together. There are over one hundred different vegetable varieties to see, along with perennial crops such as asparagus, sea kale and Jerusalem artichokes, and flowers both for cutting and attracting insect pollinators. Wooden-framed glasshouses protect warmth-loving crops like aubergines, chillies, cucumbers and tomatoes, and a patio display provides inspiration for growing edibles in containers.

Everything grown in the Herb Garden is edible, be it seeds, roots, flowers or leaves, or even the whole plant. There is also a display of different types of thyme and mint, alongside herbs for eating, seasoning and infusing. One corner is dedicated to forty different plants that can be used to make tea, from *Camellia sinensis* (common tea) to bay, cornflower and parsley. In winter, the Herb Garden becomes a framework of shrubby evergreen herbs like sage, rosemary and thyme.

Based on an original concept by Dutch garden designer Piet Oudolf in 2001, the magnificently long Glasshouse Borders stretch

from the Viewing Mount at the top end down to the Glasshouse itself. Mostly filled with North American prairie species, each border is laid out in diagonal strips or 'rivers', with three varieties of plants in each. Over the years, many plants have been replaced, but the plan remains faithful to Oudolf's style and his philosophy of naturalistic horticulture. There is still a strong emphasis on grasses and perennials that thrive with little intervention in this free-draining, nutrient-poor ground. Plants are left to grow as they would in the wild, without staking, feeding or irrigation. In summer they take on a blue-purple hue with drifts of cool colours complemented by pinkish tones and soft white flowers. In mid-autumn, shimmering grasses are the main attraction, along with the graceful, fading seed heads of herbaceous perennials.

Far left: Visitors assessing potential AGM plants on the Trials field at Wisley. Which would they choose?

Left, above: The Mediterranean Beds have been created in a large area of terraces next to the trial beds. On hot sunny days, the air is filled with the fragrance of aromatic plants.

Left, below: If you would love to visit one of the world's alpine zones but have never had the chance, walk through the Alpine Meadow instead.

Above: In spring the orchard is filled with clouds of glorious white blossom and the hum of industrious bees.

## Student digs

When the laboratory first opened in 1907, it was intended to be home for a School of Horticulture. The RHS still welcomes horticultural students, and the RHS Level 4 Diploma in Horticultural Practice provided at Wisley still remains highly prized in the industry. Over the two-year course, students work in each of the garden's departments and are expected to pass both theoretical and practical exams to prove their overall competence. While working in the garden they undertake many jobs like tidying pond plants and waterlilies in the Long Ponds, alongside more highly skilled tasks such as grafting. After such varied training they are fully prepared for a successful career in horticulture.

The pale parchment and bronze of autumnal herbaceous plants in the Glasshouse Borders are a perfect complement to the richer tones of the trees and shrubs beyond.

The landscape that sweeps dramatically around the Glasshouse itself was designed by Tom Stuart-Smith and laid out in 2007. Its flowing beds are filled with herbaceous plants constrained by clipped beech. The design links the interior plantings in the Glasshouse with the wider garden, and some of the woodland planting is reminiscent of nearby Oakwood. The green and lush scheme becomes more dry and arid-looking towards the west, mirroring that of the interior planting in the Glasshouse's dry temperate zone – a prairie meadow featuring plants native to South Africa, which was added in 2018.

The Glasshouse was a huge project for the RHS, built to celebrate the society's bicentenary in 2004. It was officially opened by Queen Elizabeth in 2007, and since that time thousands of schoolchildren have passed through and visited the attached learning centre to learn about plants and experience the pleasure of gardening.

Inside the Glasshouse are three climatic zones, showcasing plants that are difficult to grow, rare and endangered. There are also plenty of familiar 'houseplants'. The first area is the moist temperate zone, on the shadier, east side of the building. Heated to 8–12°C/46–53°F with high humidity, here visitors will find a wide range of plants from the temperate rainforests of South America and Australasia. Ferns and ground-cover plants form a carpet beneath shrubs and epiphytes, shaded by a canopy of trees and Australasian tree ferns. South American climbers and lilies, North American pitcher plants and Asian gingers grow close to a waterfall that adds a touch of the subtropical and the evocative sound of running water.

The dry temperate zone with its scree and rock-strewn landscape replicates semi-desert and desert environments. Sparsely planted, it contains a rich diversity of tough, slow-growing, often prickly plants with a strange beauty, each one of them able to survive by conserving every available drop of moisture. Desert cacti and succulents and other drought-tolerant plants from countries as far apart as Chile and Madagascar, the Canary Islands and Australia, thrive in this seemingly hostile atmosphere.

At the other end of the scale lies the tropical zone, characterised by heat, humidity and lush, leafy plants like palm trees, bananas, bromeliads and fast-growing climbers. Visitors are amazed to see the size of familiar houseplants like devil's ivy (*Epipremnum aureum*), and tropical waterlilies and other aquatic and wetland plants bask in the warm jungle pool. Occasionally, vibrantly coloured species of exotic butterflies fly freely around the tropical zone, including the blue morpho butterfly (*Morpho peleides*), with its iridescent blue wings. This special event is extremely popular in the winter months.

In any traditional, long-established garden with high numbers of visitors and a good reputation, there can be a tendency to keep things ticking over. That is not where Wisley finds itself today. Change is both welcomed and encouraged. The aim is to bring in the crowds by adding new attractions, like the Exotic Garden and the new-style Heather Landscape. Over 120,000 crocuses now illuminate the Conifer Lawn with broad swathes of purple and white in spring. New winter garden plantings on Seven Acres create a strong seasonal focal point for the area.

The mindset within the garden has been transformed under the curatorship of Matthew Pottage. There is a more dynamic outlook and staff are brimming with ideas. The creation of many new features in the garden are the result of team discussions, and

Left: The Riverside Garden, which opened in 2017 near the Pinetum, is an ideal place to stop for a picnic. Perhaps you will be lucky and see some of the rich wildlife that both Wisley and the River Wye have to offer.

Top: The inspirational pre-fabricated Glasshouse at Wisley, made of curved glass and steel was designed by Dutch architect Peter van der Toorn Vrijthoff.

Above: Alpine plants are grown under glass primarily to protect them from winter wet. In their native habitat they would be protected under a soft duvet of snow.

Right: The light and airy spaces when the Glasshouse was first constructed were soon filled with the flowers and foliage of exotic plants.

Far left: The west part of the Walled Garden at RHS Garden Wisley highlights the important impact of foliage in the structure of a garden.

Left: Caught in a moment. Once the sun has risen and the mist has evaporated, this romantic view across Seven Acres lake, through the Chinese Pagoda, will disappear.

Below: During the Christmas 'Glow' celebration, the Glasshouse shines pink and purple and blue.

an active five-year plan is also in place to help all staff gain a sense of ownership and direction, making Wisley a happy place to work.

A garden that once seemed impervious to change is now on the move. The investment project will revitalise Wisley (see pages 30–31), offering visitors even more to see and do. From the moment they step into the new 'welcome' landscape designed by Christopher Bradley-Hole, their Wisley experience will be completely transformed. For the first time in decades there will be a real dilemma in deciding what to see first – the displays in the old Laboratory, or the three fabulous new gardens around the National Centre for Horticultural Science and Learning? This really is world-class horticulture in the making.

## Close encounter

A blue morpho butterfly, one of the largest and most beautiful species in the world, shows off the beauty of its wings while resting on a leaf at 'Butterflies in the Glasshouse' at Wisley. During this celebration, thousands of visitors enjoy the magic of walking among exotic foliage and beautiful floating butterflies. Special events like this are not only an essential source of income to the RHS but also attract a new audience into their world of plants. It is also an important educational opportunity, where people of all ages can link butterflies to their food sources and habitats and be reminded of the importance of plants once again.

Autumn colour at Wisley always creates a spectacular display, particularly where it is reflected in water. It is a season when even deciduous plants of the dullest green can have their brightest moment of glory.

When it comes to Britain in Bloom, villagers at Elswick, in Lancashire, are seasoned campaigners. Attention to detail and teamwork are the recipe for success, and they have a string of gold medals to prove it.

# Chapter 4

# Gardening for all

# Gardening for all

Scientific evidence has proved conclusively that gardening is not simply a relaxing hobby. It makes a tangible contribution to society, improving the environment, communities and people's lives. At a time when mental health problems are increasing, gardening provides mindfulness, companionship, physical exercise and an opportunity to reconnect with nature. British doctors are being urged to prescribe more time outside and fewer pills. This is where the RHS fits in. As a charity that supports gardening for all, it must reflect and respond to the needs of wider society and extend its reach into urban areas and schools. One way of achieving this is through nationwide campaigns and initiatives.

The Campaign for School Gardening encourages children and teachers to discover the excitement of the natural world, using school gardens as an outdoor classroom to awaken their interest and curiosity. It also hopes to instil an understanding of why we need to take care of the environment, an outlook that students can share with others and carry with them into their adult lives.

The Britain in Bloom, It's Your Neighbourhood and Greening Grey Britain campaigns provide different ways for people to enhance their communities, both through their own gardens or growing spaces, and by joining (or creating) a local greening project. Collective efforts to improve local surroundings, making them a more beautiful place for everyone to live, can be an empowering experience for all involved. Gardening at home and in the community also creates a sense of ownership and pride. It breaks down barriers of age and race, fosters friendships and strengthens community ties. It reinforces values such as self-respect, sharing, and responsibility. For teenagers in particular, gardening provides direction and an outlet for physical energy, diverting it towards something constructive.

An inspiring example of community gardening in action is the Little Angel's Park project in the Angell Town estate, London, where local residents joined together to plant up borders using flowers donated from the RHS Chelsea Flower Show. What was once an uninviting patch of grass is now a source of enjoyment, and the park continues to be cared for by a local group, with regular RHS input.

A more recent introduction, National Gardening Week, turns the spotlight on the pleasures of gardening. A wide range of events are held across the UK, and many people join in the celebration with their own local activity or project. This is the perfect time to discover new gardens, learn practical skills and get growing.

RHS community campaigns go out to people on their home ground, helping them to use the opportunities gardening provides for their own benefit and for the benefit of those around them. The RHS has already begun to deliver on its vision to enrich everyone's life through plants, and its involvement in community gardening is set to grow and grow.

# Rocket science

## THE CAMPAIGN FOR SCHOOL GARDENING

The Big Soup Share, launched in 2017, encourages schools to turn the vegetables they grow into soup to enjoy with others. Some cook up a meal for the gardening club or the whole school; others go a step further and host a festive occasion for the local community, creating a link from plot to plate. Whatever the scale of event, this is a way for schools to celebrate their gardening achievements: the RHS even provides a template for bunting. Participation has been high. At the last count, more than 57,000 delicious bowlfuls had been served across Britain.

As part of the RHS Campaign for School Gardening, the soup share is just one among a wealth of initiatives, resources, competitions and special events designed to turn each school garden into a life-enhancing educational resource. Around 70 per cent of UK primary schools and 80 per cent of secondary schools are currently signed up. The campaign has more than 37,000 members, and welcomes not only schools but smaller organisations such as youth groups, clubs, nurseries and childminders. Although the majority have a dedicated garden, others take part using pots, raised beds or land on a local allotment.

The purpose of the campaign is to give every child the chance to try their hand at gardening, boosting their development on many levels at the same time. Teachers have easy access to information through the RHS website (rhs.org.uk/schoolgardening), where they can select from hundreds of downloadable activities, information sheets and lesson plans tailored to meet teachers' needs and complement the national curriculum. Materials range from easy-to-grow herbs and flowers from Shakespeare's plays to provision for gardening for students with special educational needs.

Training courses run by the RHS help those involved in teaching to improve their horticultural skills and make the most of their school gardens. Subjects range from how to apply maths and English skills outdoors to running a school gardening club year-round; and from edible gardening to willow art. Explorify in the Garden is based on the Wellcome Trust's innovative approach to teaching science, and is the sort of new input that encourages schools to keep on using their gardens, so they go from strength to strength.

As for pupils, an element of friendly competition helps generate interest. Incentives include RHS Young School Gardener of the Year (awarded in 2018 to dynamic fifteen-year-old Ellie Micklewright from Shropshire) and Budding Gardeners, which invites schools to create miniature show gardens at Wisley. In another challenge, the RHS gave away 100 seeds harvested from a 340-kilogram/53½-stone pumpkin grown at Hyde Hall by vegetable expert Matthew Oliver. The seeds went to campaign members around the UK, to see who could grow the biggest monster by the end of summer 2018. The winner was Deer Park Primary School, Chesterfield, for their 110-kilogram/17-stone entry.

No doubt, the most exciting project so far for teenagers was the Rocket Science experiment run by the RHS in partnership with the UK Space Agency. One million seeds (or 2 kilograms/4½ pounds) of salad rocket were launched on Soyuz 44S with British astronaut Tim Peake, arriving on the International Space Station on 4 September 2015. After about six months the seeds were returned to earth and distributed to over 8,600 schools and groups, each one also receiving an equal quantity of ordinary rocket seeds. The two packets were unmarked but colour coded, red and blue: the objective was to observe differences in germination and growth, feeding the results into a national online

database. This got participants thinking about the challenges of growing crops on long space voyages or even on another planet.

Data provided by the 600,000 young scientists revealed that the space seeds – after being subject to violent vibrations while breaking clear of the earth's gravitational pull, microgravity, fluctuating temperatures and space radiation – only grew marginally less well. This shows how seeds that have survived both the rigours of a journey to space and being stored for several months are still viable, and can germinate and grow.

More recently, I Can Grow has encouraged young people to use plants as a way to campaign for a cause of their choosing. The RHS Green Plan It challenge, run for the third year in 2018, is a ten-week schools' garden design competition that sees teams of 12–14-year-olds working with a mentor from the horticultural industry to develop imaginative designs for a new garden for their school or community. This gives young people an insight into the importance of plants in our everyday lives and raises awareness of horticultural career options.

Stories gathered from schools show just what can be achieved. Heron Hill Primary School in Kendal, Cumbria, is an inspiring example. Around 2.6 hectares/6½ acres of grassland have been transformed into a stimulating setting for children to explore, featuring a Quiet Garden, hedgehog houses, a composting area and over 2,000 native trees. Pupils have been involved in the design, plant choice and construction, often enlisting family support by bringing plants from home. Each year-group now has a section of the garden to look after independently, their efforts backed up by a weekly gardening club that keeps going whatever the weather. Accompanied by parents and volunteers, the club embarks on a new challenge every year. The garden is used as an outdoor classroom for all ages and for fun events like Easter egg trails.

It also serves a therapeutic purpose as an outlet for children feeling overwhelmed by circumstances or who find formal learning difficult, particularly those with autism. And that's not all: a group of children are keeping bees as a self-financing enterprise.

Gardening is a powerful tool with wide-ranging benefits, as the RHS campaign is proving. It enhances literacy, numeracy and language skills, and enriches the whole school curriculum. It improves health and wellbeing, builds life skills such as confidence, teamwork and communication, and informs young people about the environment, helping them to better engage with their surroundings and develop a sense of responsibility. With more than a decade of experience behind its inventive campaign, the RHS aims to bring these benefits to an ever-widening circle of young people.

Above: In schools, hanging gloves on a clothes line is a great way to ensure that they dry out and always stay as pairs. Watering cans are often brightly coloured too; there is less chance of losing a red one.

Right, top: The Schools Wheelbarrow Competition first appeared at the RHS Flower Show in Cardiff in 2014, and has remained popular ever since. Each barrow is full of ideas.

Right, bottom: A pupil at Hammersmith Academy, winners of the RHS School Gardening Team of the Year 2017 award, helps reinforce the link between plants and the care they need.

Left: There is a stark contrast between the sterility of a close-mown verge and a nectar-filled flowery meadow, which is beneficial to pollinators.

Right: Paddock Allotments at Raynes Park won London Allotment Site of the Year at the London in Bloom awards, 2011. It's easy to see why.

# Flower power

## BRITAIN IN BLOOM

Britain in Bloom, which has been running for more than fifty years, is the UK's favourite gardening competition and one of the largest of its kind in Europe. It involves more than 1,300 communities, each striving to make their city, town or village a cleaner, greener and more beautiful place to live. Impressive floral displays with bedding and hanging baskets were once central to the competition, and still provide the wow factor, but today an almost equal importance is given to long-term planting. The Britain in Bloom remit has become broader in the last couple of decades to reflect contemporary concerns, with the result that many Bloom groups find that taking part helps build stronger communities, tackle social issues and protect the environment. Examples of the far-reaching impact of Britain in Bloom include growing fresh fruit and vegetables to stock community fridges and supplement food parcels for families in need, and protecting vulnerable species such as the small blue butterfly through the conservation of natural habitats.

The competition was first held in 1963, initiated by the British Tourist Board at the suggestion of horticultural journalist Roy Hay, who had seen flower-filled villages while on holiday in France. Since 2001 the RHS has been working in partnership with the Bloom Federation of regions and nations to deliver the UK-wide programme, ensuring its continuing popularity. A survey in 2015 showed that 300,000 Bloom volunteers were donating millions of hours to community projects. To join in, community gardening groups involved in activities such as planting up local streets, school gardening or caring for a park, can register to compete on a regional level. The most successful areas are then put through to the national RHS Britain in Bloom finals, which are held the following year. In 2018, seventy-six entries contended for the top awards. Viewers of the BBC Two series *Britain in Bloom*, presented by Chris Bavin, enjoyed following participants as they prepare for judging day with infectious positivity.

Evaluation concentrates on three core areas – horticultural achievement, environmental responsibility and community participation – and standards are high. On judging day, groups provide a guided tour with stopping points carefully tailored to show off their efforts, but the judges are in fact assessing the horticultural quality of all they see *en route*, in front gardens, community centres, car parks and pubs. Nothing escapes their eagle eyes and the questions they ask are wide-ranging. Are the colours, design and plant choice suitable for the location? Has the campaign been active throughout the year? What efforts are being made to engage a wide range of people across all areas of the community?

Oldham's Bloom and Grow campaign has been active since 2000 and has won multiple awards, including Gold in the Champion of Champions category of the 2017 national finals. There is no doubt that success of this kind boosts civic pride, but Britain in Bloom is about more than winning medals. Communities may notice a positive effect on the local economy through increased tourism and investment, as well as less tangible benefits like a greater sense of ownership. In fact, community gardening can breathe new life into an area.

With a nursery growing around 160,000 plants for spring and summer bedding, Oldham's Bloom and Grow is a big horticultural operation; but its real strength lies in its wide-ranging programme

of community involvement, reaching out even to people who do not think of themselves as gardeners. Education is a priority, so young people are involved in planting days and environmental campaigns. A training programme run in conjunction with the local college helps unemployed people find long-term work. For the wider public, community-run growing hubs dotted around the town provide a venue for fun-oriented gardening sessions that also help build skills. Through its Green Dividend scheme, Bloom and Grow provides grants so community groups can create growing spaces and allotments. Dull, disused alleyways behind terraced houses are turned into communal areas to grow plants, becoming social spaces where people can meet and chat. This helps combat loneliness, improves health and wellbeing, and reduces antisocial problems like fly-tipping and graffiti. An annual public health grant of nearly £500,000 allows further schemes to be developed as a direct result of Oldham's Bloom success.

Bury in Bloom is another town taking a holistic approach to improve the quality of life for residents. It has won Gold fourteen consecutive times in the North West in Bloom regional contest, represented the region six times nationally, and in 2017 was joint winner of the discretionary Overcoming Adversity award for the way the council workforce and community tackled vandalism with unwavering resolve. The town is proud of how Bury in Bloom fosters cooperation, as groups of all ages join forces to work towards a common goal. They see their success as the sum of all the initiatives going on at different levels, including the schoolchildren who have turned a disused bowling green into a wildlife-friendly space using raised planters, bug hotels and plants for pollinators. Householders can help by taking a street-care pledge to litter-pick in their area,

> 'What better way to integrate yourself with your neighbours and fellow members of the community, than working together to make it a better place for everyone?'

which in turn develops community pride. Another project, in partnership with the Bury Council ground maintenance team, seeks to include people living with disabilities or affected by social disadvantage; through volunteering to grow plants for the town's hanging baskets they can develop work skills and confidence.

As an advocate of community gardening, the RHS values Britain in Bloom for the wider social, economic and environmental benefits it brings. The programme is in constant development to ensure it stays relevant; in 2018 a new category for town and city centres was added, in recognition of the vital role of green spaces in urban areas. Of course, having fun is a big part of the experience. Presenter Chris Bavin agrees: 'What better way to integrate yourself with your neighbours and fellow members of the community, than working together to make it a better place for everyone?'

Left: This simple display of *Perovskia* and *Echinacea* at the Open University in Milton Keynes is both attractive and a rich food source for pollinators.

Above: Raised beds mean that even tarmacked areas are a useful place to grow plants. Now, what shall we grow up that lovely brick wall?

Top: Whatever the space, plants will green it up. This community border flourishing next to Kensington House, Bristol, planted by St George in Bloom, demonstrates exactly how it's done.

Right: Flower beds created as part of the Greening the Gorbals Project run by the Gorbals Healthy Living Network in Glasgow.

# Community gardening

## IT'S YOUR NEIGHBOURHOOD

Introduced in 2006, the RHS It's Your Neighbourhood (IYN) initiative is a non-competitive and informal offshoot of Britain in Bloom that offers a way of making new friends while joining local volunteers to clean and green up a chosen area. Any space counts, however large or small. It could be a street, a bus stop, the corner of a park or a litter-filled wasteland. Around the UK, nearly 2,000 projects are transforming and strengthening communities through gardening, each one with its own particular story to tell. Here are just a few: the urban nature wonderland in Tower Hamlets Cemetery Park, London; a green refuge designed and managed by homeless people next to Glasgow Central train station; and a multicultural gardening club in Reading, which grows Nepalese crops to share with the community.

The ability of gardening to unite seemingly disparate groups is highlighted by a project in Hereford. When a new skatepark opened in 2008, plot holders on the nearby Holmer Allotments were wary of the youngsters arriving from all over the country with their hoodies, scooters and pimped-up skateboards. They expected noise, vandalism and antisocial behaviour. A series of burglaries that occurred soon after the park was opened seemed to confirm their worst fears, although these were later found to be unconnected with users of the skatepark.

Allotmenteer Sharon Baugh, who walked past the skatepark every day, could not help noticing how much enjoyment it provided. She also noticed that the site was very exposed, with no shade, shelter or windbreaks. Coincidentally, the allotment had recently been invited to become more involved with Hereford in Bloom, which Sharon saw as an ideal opportunity to break down barriers by working with the skatepark on a joint community project under the IYN banner.

With the support of friends, and a donation of trees and bamboo plants, Sharon formed an IYN group in 2012. She found that the kids from the skatepark were happy to lend a hand. On an agreed date, eighteen young boarders and seven plot holders turned up to prepare and plant. It was a resounding success, especially since the different generations found they had more in common than they imagined. The first planting event led to Digging Boarders, a group that met monthly to pool ideas and make plans. A grant from Herefordshire Council allowed them to buy plants, fruit trees and bird boxes, and in autumn 2018 there were masses of plums for the skateboarders to feast on.

Although IYN projects are very diverse, they share the same set of values as Britain in Bloom, set out under three headings by the RHS. One is community participation. This can take many forms but hinges on local people taking charge and making decisions for the benefit of their community. Raising support, planning for the future and working in partnership with other organisations are elements of a thriving project. The aim is for everyone involved, whatever their age, circumstances or personal background, to feel welcome. Contributions can include lending resources and giving moral support as well as hands-on gardening.

Environmental responsibility is another strand, covering all the different ways you can care for your locality. The goal might be to reduce graffiti and fly-tipping. It might be to encourage the use of peat-free compost, improve green spaces, or make bird boxes. Efforts

Above: Local volunteers clear litter and weeds in Walthamstow Village Square, East London, to make sure that everything looks immaculate for the Bloom competition. A community that gardens together creates a strong sense of ownership and pride; public green spaces belong to us all.

Opposite: This RHS outreach project, working with the charity Young Saheliya in Glasgow, greened up the grey courtyard at the centre where they met. Brightly coloured containers provided instant sunshine, and trellis provided opportunities to grow plants vertically. Greening up an area doesn't have to be costly. Think recycled materials and you will soon be on your way.

Right: In 2003, a member of Organiclea, a group promoting locally grown organic food in north-east London, noticed that there were lots of apple trees with fruit that was left unpicked, so their Scrumping Project was born. Much of the fruit harvested by volunteers arrives at the Hornbeam Community Centre in environmentally friendly bicycle trailers.

Right, bottom left: Over the centuries, apples have been planted in many parks or as street trees in London. Victorian architect John Warner, who built many of Walthamstow's local houses on an old orchard, put apples or pears in every garden. The most common variety is the 'Lisley Crab' (or 'Walthamstow Pink' to the locals).

Right, bottom right: A portable press is used for street pressings and the public are invited to take part. The 'pomace', or pulp, that remains is composted.

to share knowledge and skills are included here, as well as heritage-related activities like tree trails and interpretation boards, which can reinforce a sense of belonging.

Of utmost importance is gardening achievement, which covers good horticultural practice appropriate to local needs and conditions. The quality of maintenance comes in here, such as pruning and weeding, but also the creative choice of plants, solving site difficulties and organising community activities like planting events.

Britain in Bloom supports IYN by sending out regional mentors and, once a year, assessors, whose role is not to judge but to encourage, monitor progress and provide constructive feedback so the group can make an even greater impact. The national network formed by IYN is reflected in the quarterly RHS magazine *Grass Roots*, which is dedicated to community gardening and filled with inspirational stories and expert advice. There is also a regular presence on social media, offering opportunities for groups to help each other out.

Each new group sets its own goals on joining the scheme. At first, these generally revolve around planning, consulting local people and recruiting volunteers. Then, as the group increases in number and gains experience, the focus shifts to getting the job done. Projects often evolve beyond initial expectations, as in Dundee, where a bee-friendly wildflower meadow was created to cheer up a derelict community garden. It began with a 'guerrilla' gardening exercise by Grove Academy's sixth-year students, who in 2009 cleared the site of litter and hardcore, later making clandestine raids to scatter compost and seeds. The project rapidly expanded, pioneered by members of the school's Eco Group and other adult or youth volunteers. New features are added every year. In 2012, the city's Community Payback

Team came to build a raised bed for herbs, and the Nature Nutters, a local young environmentalists' group, created a bug hotel, gabion planters and a woodchip path. A grant from Volunteering Matters has led to a new wildlife pond and seating area filled with sensory plants. More recently, Grove Academy pupils helped put up butterfly mosaics made at the Douglas Community Centre, and the latest autumn clear-up added spring bulbs for 2019. The group regularly takes part in local and national initiatives, including the Ribbon of Poppies campaign and the Broughty Ferry Scarecrow Trail. More creative ideas are coming soon. Here in Queen Street, Dundee and in communities all around the UK, people are joining together through IYN and improving the places where they live.

# Up front with gardening

## GREENING GREY BRITAIN CAMPAIGN

Front gardens and patios across the country are being transformed as people take up the Greening Grey Britain challenge. The movement, originally started to reverse the total paving over of front gardens, is gaining momentum, spreading out into unloved spaces in local neighbourhoods, empty concrete-covered corners and ugly alleyways, bare school playgrounds and uninviting slabs of tarmac in front of shops. Cold, dark expanses of paving are changing into green beacons that enrich human lives, benefit wildlife and improve the environment.

Anywhere there is space to plant counts. Some people add a tree or a climber. Others choose a flower bed or window box. No spot is too small, as each contributes to the bigger picture. Community gardening projects are also sprouting up in response to the campaign, pooling skills and imagination in the quest to turn grey areas green. The RHS is almost halfway to its goal of 6,000 pledges from participating groups and individuals.

The initiative began to emerge in 2011, after RHS scientists joined with colleagues at the universities of Reading and Sheffield to review evidence from around the world about the impact of domestic gardens on the quality of urban life. What they discovered was that plants have greater positive effects than was previously thought. While impermeable paving puts city homes at increased risk of flooding through rainwater run-off, plants intercept heavy rain, and the soil they live in absorbs water, combining to relieve pressure on drains. Gardens contribute to biodiversity in cities, acting as miniature nature reserves. Human health and wellbeing also improve when there are more opportunities for interaction with green spaces.

The RHS study revealed another important role for garden plants: they help regulate temperatures in cities. Pavements and roads absorb heat during the day and release this energy at night, contributing to a phenomenon called the urban heat island effect, which explains why cities are often warmer than surrounding rural areas. Plants, on the other hand, act as a form of air conditioning by cooling the air with their shade and with water evaporating from pores in their leaves. Having plants in cities makes hot weather more bearable and could reduce the effects of higher temperatures due to climate change.

Climbing plants are a natural form of insulation for buildings, creating a layer of still air between the vegetation and external wall surface. This can reduce the cost of cooling by an estimated 30 per cent. Trees and hedges carefully placed around houses to form windbreaks can also save on energy for heating. Hedges, particularly of conifers, have additional benefits, as they are known to filter pollution effectively from nearby roads. More generally, plants improve air quality by absorbing carbon dioxide and releasing oxygen.

Although small individually, gardens throughout Britain represent a colossal amount of green space and this cumulative area has a considerable impact on people and ecosystems. Domestic gardens can make a real difference – yet RHS scientists were alarmed to discover that much of Britain is being paved over. Statistics relating to front gardens are particularly stark: 7 million front gardens are partially paved over and another 5 million (around one in four) contain no plants at all. Three times more front gardens are paved over compared to the situation a decade ago, usually for off-street parking. The worst affected location is London, where nearly half of front gardens have been completely paved.

The RHS concluded that planting up and protecting urban gardens can have a significant impact on individual homes and the wider environment, making cities better places to live, which is why they launched their campaign in 2015. The 2017 Chelsea Flower Show presented an occasion to illustrate what could be achieved by taking a fresh approach. Nigel Dunnett, professor of planting design and vegetation technology at the University of Sheffield and RHS ambassador for Greening Grey Britain, designed a modern garden brimming with ecological ideas set in the context of a high-rise apartment block. His low-input, high-impact planting style aimed to create a long-lasting, colourful display with good wildlife value. (The garden also contained the first ever display of street art in the flower show's history.)

In parallel, a multidisciplinary group, including town planners and doctors, met to discuss the challenges ahead, in what was termed the Front Garden Summit. It was clear from this that more research was needed, so the RHS stepped in to help. Lauriane Suyin Chalmin-Pui, an RHS-sponsored PhD student at the University of Sheffield, began to examine the therapeutic effects of front gardens in greater detail, with help from the occupants of a street in Salford.

New information is continually being gathered to update the advice provided by Greening Grey Britain, which offers simple solutions and design ideas for all, based on readily available, easy-to-grow plants that have been endorsed with the RHS Award of Garden Merit or deemed beneficial for pollinators. Visitors to the RHS website can find helpful videos (showing, for example, how front gardens can happily accommodate both parking and plants) as well as details of the latest inspiring success stories. One of the

> 'Although small individually, gardens throughout Britain represent a colossal amount of green space and this cumulative area has a considerable impact on people and ecosystems.'

most heartening has been the transformation achieved at the Angell Town estate in Brixton, south London (see pages 74–7).

Anyone who wants to take part in the campaign can make an online promise to help, sharing their progress through social media as an encouragement to others. If adding a single tree or shrub makes a difference, imagine what planting a whole garden with a diverse range of plants can achieve, or creating a green roof or a rain garden. Greening Grey Britain is about reclaiming the grey, and the RHS is committed to help everyone, one plant at a time.

Left: 'Come on everyone, let's get together and green up our space.' It takes people, plants and enthusiasm to make a project work. This local resident is watering new plants at a playground in Walthamstow Village.

Above: The RHS promoted Greening Grey Britain at the Chelsea Flower Show in 2017. The garden, designed by Professor Nigel Dunnett (seen here watering the plants), was full of practical ideas for visitors to take home.

Right, top: This funky front garden, with its tiny lawn and attendant lions, is filled with colourful bedding. The tree by the window, nature's net curtains, provides privacy, too. Front gardens are important for those who pass by; a little splash of colour can brighten someone's day.

Right, bottom: Filling every inch of a front garden with greenery creates a barrier between the path and the house, deters intruders and is an invaluable habitat for wildlife.

Left: A dull green space was transformed into a beautiful living painting when the Chelsea Flower Show garden designed by Ann-Marie Powell in 2016 was transplanted to Little Angel's Park on the Angell Town estate in Brixton.

Right: Pretty yet practical, *Geranium phaeum* var. *phaeum* 'Samobor', with purple-blotched leaves, flourishes in dry shade.

# Gardening changes lives

## COMMUNITY GARDEN IN LONDON

When David Cohen wrote the first in a series of hard-hitting articles in the *Evening Standard* about life on the Angell Town estate in Brixton, little did he know that gardening, of all things, would offer a source of hope. His report, which appeared in September 2015, followed a special investigation and made some alarming revelations. The estate had a long history of gang violence, both within the estate and turf wars involving rival gangs. More than half the estate was living in poverty and the Department for Communities and Local Government classed it among the most deprived areas in the country. Cohen described Angell Town as a parallel world, far removed from the London he moved around in. His third day on the estate ended in a shooting.

Some members of the community wanted to break the cycle of violence, but previous attempts to improve the lives of families had failed. There was a move to start a boxing club to keep the younger generation occupied, except there was nowhere for the club to meet. Children did not play outdoors. The only flowers on view were the bouquets tied to the railings 30 metres/100 feet from the local park to mark the spot where a young man had been murdered. If only things could change.

As a result of Cohen's articles, the *Evening Standard* launched The Estate We're In, a programme of support for community-led initiatives to tackle social problems. Focusing on the positive potential of London's deprived housing estates, the aim was to empower residents 'by responding to issues they identify as important and ideas they have for generating improvement in

their neighbourhood'. The Angell Town estate became the pilot scheme, with financial backing from the local authority, several city corporations and the Evening Standard Dispossessed Fund. If successful, the newspaper planned to roll the programme out to other troubled estates.

Meanwhile, the RHS was working to increase awareness of the beneficial effects that gardening and the presence of plants can have on people's health and happiness. From Cohen's articles, it was clear to many that there was a connection to be made between the Angell Town estate and the then newly launched Greening Grey Britain campaign (see pages 70–73). As a result, the RHS decided to join forces with residents and the *Evening Standard* to see if a positive change could be brought about in the community through gardening.

It began with the Chelsea Flower Show, which, as a high-profile event, can be an effective way of bringing issues to a wider audience. In 2016 the urban garden designed for the show by Ann-Marie Powell celebrated the value of plants in cities and incorporated ideas for using recycled materials. It was full of colour, radiating energy and lifting the spirits through a recurring theme of orange and purple. Every surface was filled with planting; even the potting shed roof was packed with containers of cacti and California poppies. Plants grown by Angell Town residents were incorporated into the garden and six residents helped build it. After the show, it was dismantled and the plants transferred to Little Angel's Park as part of a longer-term greening project involving a local gardening group.

Before the garden was relocated to its new site, five months of consultation had already established the needs of Angell Town

Top: The 'RHS Feel Good Garden' by Matt Keightley, at the Chelsea Flower Show in 2018, demonstrated how soft colours like blue and green can create a soothing sense of calm, even at the heart of a bustling flower show.

Left: Orange energy beams out from a shipping container in the 'RHS Greening Grey Britain Garden' in 2016, as its designer Ann-Marie Powell wonders what the fuss is all about.

Right: When everyone had lent a hand, and the Little Angel's Park on the Angell Town estate had been planted, it was officially opened by Mayor of London Sadiq Khan.

residents through questionnaires, open days and leafleting. (The shipping container potting shed was declined.) At the park, turf was removed and flower beds shaped so that planting could begin. The Chelsea lupins, alliums, geums and roses arrived, as well as donations of other plants and tools. Celebrated floral decorator Simon Lycett and Chelsea Gold-medallist Matt Keightley, known for garden designs centred on wellbeing, worked alongside RHS volunteers and enthusiastic residents for three rainy but highly satisfying days in June 2016. Even people who did not live on the estate turned up to lend a hand. Grandparents mingled with teenagers and infants, and people who had never met before began to chat and help one another. For those involved, it was a chance to connect with other people and with the soil.

The little pocket park was transformed from a sad, colourless sweep of rough grass into a flower-filled jewel of a garden that immediately became a source of local pride. When all the work was done, the park was officially opened by the mayor of London, Sadiq Khan, who planted the final rose. This inspiring project continues to benefit the community as local volunteers and schoolchildren meet to maintain the park, coordinated by Simon Ghartey of the community support company Progess London. Other groups are involved from time to time, including the young offenders' projects that have constructed garden benches and planters, and volunteers on loan from city companies that opt to sponsor corporate social responsibility days. The RHS regularly provides advice and expertise.

Since 2016, the experience of enlisting community support at Angell Town has informed the way other RHS Chelsea Flower Show gardens are relocated. Two gardens with a health and wellbeing theme recently went to good homes at Burlais Primary School in Swansea, which was in need of colour for its grey courtyard, and Highgate Mental Health Centre, located in a built-up part of London where green space is limited.

It is no exaggeration to say that gardening changes lives. The last words go to Sadiq Khan: 'The great thing about a garden is that it democratises the space. It turns passive citizens into active citizens, gives them a sense of shared pride and sends a powerful signal that "you matter". I saw such happiness here — four generations of local families, different ethnicities, faiths, all coming together around a garden.'

# Seven days to celebrate

## NATIONAL GARDENING WEEK

Britain's biggest celebration of gardening was launched in spring 2012 to get the nation growing and looking beautiful. The week offers something for everyone, and everyone's invited to host and attend a wide range of events. Members of the public, garden owners and nurseries, youth clubs, schools, community groups, associations and charities, businesses, museums and heritage sites all regularly take part in this increasingly popular festival, which mobilises the enthusiasm of thousands of people in support of gardening. It is a great chance for young families and beginner gardeners to get out and about exploring gardens they may never have seen before, and to benefit from a host of special activities designed to help and inspire. There is naturally plenty to interest the more experienced as well, who are encouraged to share their love of gardening through local events so that others can take their horticultural skills a step further.

The RHS, which came up with the initiative, proposes several ways to get involved: by going along to one of the events from the nationwide programme; by hosting your own local event such as a garden party; or simply by getting stuck into a horticultural project at home. National Gardening Week celebrates all that is wonderful about gardens, revolving around a different theme each year, and RHS gardens lead the way with an array of activities. When the focus was on how gardens and gardening keep us fit, RHS Garden Wisley offered fitness classes incorporating – surely for the first time in its history – an organised buggy push around Seven Acres, and Wisley's horticulturists revealed how gardening keeps them happy and healthy.

Many RHS Partner Gardens join in with their own slant on the theme, and private gardens open especially for the occasion. Events take different forms, including tours, talks, exhibitions and workshops, plant fairs and clinics. Some gardens offer a glimpse behind the scenes, or reveal the secrets of how their borders are kept looking beautiful throughout the growing season. For others, the week coincides with the peak of a plant collection, such as bluebells, tulips or rhododendrons. New developments, large and small, are also unveiled: the first public viewing of a community-built sensory garden at Easington Colliery, East Durham, coincided with National Gardening Week, as did the grand opening of the restored Temperate House at the Royal Botanic Gardens, Kew.

All kinds of interest are catered for. Picture yoga among the grass borders at Knoll Gardens in Dorset, flower arranging at Holker Hall in Cumbria, minibeast hunting at Ardarden Walled Garden in Argyll and a folly family trail at Fountains Abbey, North Yorkshire. There are opportunities to hear from head gardeners, designers, garden historians and wildlife experts. Specialist plant societies offer guidance, and there is often practical advice available for people with specific needs; the Kent Association for the Blind, for instance, held a day for gardeners adapting to sight impairment. Taken as a whole, this panoply of events reflects the countless ways we experience, use and value gardens.

Over the years, National Gardening Week has introduced many participants to the essentials of gardening. There has been help choosing the correct plants for different locations, advice on understanding how soil works, and information on simple seed sowing and ways to root cuttings. Families have found out how to

Below: Gardening should be a pleasure, not a pain in the back: this gardener is showing a good weeding technique by crouching, not bending.

Bottom: Hyacinths add welcome colour and fragrance in spring and the wide path has been well thought out. When pushing a barrow, there is no chance of accidentally trampling the plants.

Right: The RHS and industry partners launched National Gardening Week in 2012 by handing out seeds to encourage the nation to get growing. Even extending to floral attire!

Opposite: Traditionally a Union Jack is bedded out in blue lobelias, white alyssums and red salvias. The RHS provided its own variation on the theme at Wisley during National Gardening Week.

'National Gardening Week celebrates all that is wonderful about gardens, revolving around a different theme each year, and RHS gardens lead the way with an array of activities.'

grow a money plant (*Crassula ovata*) from a single leaf and what to do about poorly houseplants. Others have seen how to create hanging baskets, grow vegetables in a small space or switch to environmentally friendly lawncare. Each national gardening week brings a whole new set of possibilities.

The focus is not solely on acquiring skills, however: everyone involved in National Gardening Week would like more people to take pleasure in growing plants, to benefit from being active outdoors and to enjoy engaging with nature. By fostering a shared love of gardening, it is hoped that National Gardening Week can create connections between people and lead to a wider feeling of togetherness. The event can also be a spur to action, providing the impetus needed to get involved in a local project. Amisfield Walled Garden, in East Lothian, for example, is being restored as a community garden and used the

occasion in 2018 to invite potential volunteers for a taster session. Elsewhere, participants have left their mark on the landscape by planting a carpet of 10,000 snowdrops at Killerton Garden, Devon, and by sowing wildflowers at Beach House Park in Worthing, West Sussex.

For anyone choosing to host an event of their own, the RHS suggests they register online to become part of the bigger picture, then record the experience on social media. (In 2018 the National Gardening Week hashtag was used almost 10,000 times and the topic trended on Twitter in the UK.) Popular ways to share a love of gardening include organising fun activities in a park, fundraising for a community garden or coordinating a joint effort to tidy up a neglected corner of the neighbourhood. Another way to join in the celebration is to adopt a gardening project to do at home. Lots of tempting ideas are given on the National Gardening Week website, such as building a bee hotel, creating a night-scented garden, making a log shelter or planting herbs in containers.

The first National Gardening Week was held in mid-April, but since 2018 it has been moved forward by a few weeks to the beginning of May to benefit from better weather and a greater display of colour in gardens. Now an established event in the gardening year, this lively celebration is an expression of how we value gardens and provides an occasion for people across the UK to celebrate them in pretty much any way they please.

The Cottage Garden at Rosemoor, with its massed herbaceous perennials, provides a warm welcome to visitors to the garden in summer.

# Chapter 5
# Rosemoor

Left, clockwise from top left: the lake can be a wonderful, tranquil place at any time of year; trees, shrubs and ferns combine to add daintiness and elegance to autumn; the Foliage Garden shows off varying shapes and forms and the brush-like plumes of grasses; wrap up warmly and visit the Winter Garden to enjoy *Pinus strobus* 'Louie', *Acer griseum* and *Erica carnea* in all their seasonal beauty; the Stone Garden, one of the oldest parts of the garden, was designed in 1932 by Lady Anne's mother; the Hot Garden is slightly cooled by the softer colours of the trees in the landscape beyond;

the Long Borders reveal a succession of attractive colour schemes and well-grown, beautiful plants; (left) a waterfall in the Rock Gully provides shade and running water, whatever the season; (right) work on the Rock Gully began in 1995 using nearly 500 tonnes of stone, creating the perfect home for shade lovers like bamboo and ferns; the Hot Garden borders are a sizzling mix of plants such as heleniums, lobelias and kniphofias.

Right: Lady Anne's House, with its wisteria-covered facade, remains the heart and soul of Rosemoor.

# Rosemoor

### DEVON GARDEN

Each RHS garden has its own distinctive identity, forged by the interplay between location, plants, and the continual experimentation of gardeners. Tucked into a north Devon valley near Great Torrington, Rosemoor is a garden of two parts. The newer part is known for its fruit and vegetable beds, twin rose gardens and Hot Garden, which dazzles in summer with bold blocks of colour. The older part has an intimate feel, with cherry trees blending into woodland and interesting collections of plants. Water features contribute to different moods, from the gush of the Rock Gully to the calm of the lake, and the garden's West Country roots are honoured through local materials and plants such as the Devon sorb (*Sorbus devoniensis*), a small tree with bunches of edible russet fruit.

The garden was originally created by Lady Anne Palmer, whose father bought Rosemoor as a fishing lodge. She came to live here in 1931, aged twelve. Nearly three decades later, when in Spain recovering from the measles, she happened to meet noted plantsman Collingwood 'Cherry' Ingram and a great gardening friendship began. Over the following decades she transformed a dull garden that she viewed as 'typically Victorian, with a great use of annuals in beds around the house', into a plant-collector's paradise filled with treasures from her travels to North and South America, Papua New Guinea, New Zealand and Japan. Some of her rare rhododendrons have recently been micropropagated as a way to conserve them for the future.

The growing conditions at Rosemoor are not the easiest: a clay-lined frost pocket receiving more than 1 metre/39 inches of rainfall a year. Lady Anne wisely used the sunny, sheltered microclimate of west-facing borders around the Croquet Lawn for her beautiful southern hemisphere plants, including the unmistakable monkey puzzle (*Araucaria araucana*) and less familiar perennials such as fragrant *Crinum* x *powellii* and pretty pink *Dahlia merckii*. Also near the house, visitors can enjoy the Mediterranean Garden, where California poppies self-seed among euphorbias, and the Exotic Garden, lush with hardy bananas (*Musa basjoo*), cannas and ginger lilies (*Hedychium*). Lady Anne's great interest in trees is witnessed by the arboretum she planted from the mid-1970s, raising many specimens from seed.

In 1988 Lady Anne gifted her 3.2-hectare/8-acre garden to the RHS, along with 13 hectares/32 acres of former pastureland, and emigrated to New Zealand to join her second husband, the dendrologist Bob Berry. And so the garden entered a new phase, opening to the public in June 1990. The challenge of creating a masterplan fell to Elizabeth Banks Associates, who were faced with the awkward fact that the fields and garden were separated by the A3124, running roughly north-south. The solution was to embrace the idea of two distinct areas. Visitors would arrive at a new garden developed within the pastureland, then cross by an underpass to explore Lady Anne's Garden.

Site preparations were intense. The pastureland was levelled using over 13,000 tonnes of soil relocated from construction works at the adjacent entrance and car park, and graded to create a gentle fall to the River Torridge. A small stream nearby was diverted and dammed, forming a sequence of pools and waterfalls down to a new lake holding a provision of 1.8 million litres/400,000 gallons for irrigation.

A formal garden by the new entrance building was laid out as

a series of six 'rooms' framed with yew hedging and linked by a colourful central walkway known as the Long Borders. Landscape architect Elizabeth Banks, who wanted visitors to see flowers as soon as they stepped into the garden, designed two rose gardens here, challenging the accepted wisdom that the damp West Country climate and sulphur-free air make it unsuitable for growing healthy roses. The Queen Mother's Rose Garden is planted with modern roses for scent and colour, while the Shrub Rose Garden is full of traditional Alba, Damask, Gallica and Moss roses chosen for their disease resistance, vigour and long flowering season. Both are loved by visitors and have been an outstanding success.

Gradually, each room was given its own character. The Hot Garden, with prairie-style planting, is at its best from July to mid-September, and the Cottage Garden, centred on a charming thatched summerhouse, is filled with an informal mix of hardy geraniums, aquilegias, poppies and sweet peas amid carefully placed shrubs. An ornamental potager with a circular design uses modern and heritage varieties to create patterns of colour, form and texture from foliage, fruit and edible flowers.

The open landscape nearby leads to the lake and is bisected by the Stream Garden containing a collection of water iris. At the northern boundary, beyond an orchard, is the popular Fruit and Vegetable Garden demonstrating different methods, from traditional rows to raised beds, containers and catch crops. South- and west-facing stone walls provide sheltered conditions that are ideal for peaches, nectarines and figs. Trained fruit trees and climbing annuals such as squashes are supported on split-chestnut paling, which is well adapted to the task as it allows frost to drain away.

Crossing to the other side of the garden, in an open area south of the original house, lies the Bicentenary Arboretum, planted in 2004 to commemorate 200 years of the RHS. Arranged geographically, by their region of origin, the trees here provide glorious colour in autumn to complement Lady Anne's Arboretum, which is being expanded with dogwoods (part of a National Plant Collection of *Cornus*), rhododendrons, witch hazels (*Hamamelis*) and cherries (*Prunus*) for spring colour.

For a number of years, Rosemoor has been developing links with Orchards Live, a north-Devon association determined to reverse the decline in traditional orchards and conserve locally bred apples. The idea of setting up a reference collection was aired, leading in spring 2017 to the Devon Orchard. Comprising forty-five cultivars with evocative names like 'Devon Pendragon' or 'Pig's Nose', the trees follow the curving contours of the land rather than being planted in regimented lines, and a wildflower meadow below attracts pollinators.

As in all RHS gardens, the aim is for visitors to enjoy every moment while being inspired, informed and offered ideas to take away for their own gardens. The whole of Rosemoor is a learning resource, from green manures to plants for winter scent. In addition, the Peter Buckley Learning Centre, sited south of the Formal Garden, holds curriculum-based workshops for around 7,000 primary-school pupils annually and is looking to expand into secondary education. Nearby, the community allotments provide a scheme to get beginners growing their own fruit and vegetables, with expert help from Rosemoor's edibles team. Trials are also held here to identify vegetable cultivars capable of thriving in heavy, wet conditions.

Left: If the Hot Garden gets just too hot, the soft green of the trees beyond will cool you down.

Top: Birches, ferns and camassias complement the traditional construction of this elegant wooden bridge.

Above: The flower-filled Cottage Garden is home to roses, delphiniums and other much-loved and traditional favourites.

## Garden classrooms

The Peter Buckley Learning Centre, to the south of the Formal Garden at Rosemoor, holds workshops for around 7,000 primary-school pupils annually and is looking to expand into other areas of education. The whole of the Formal Garden is bounded by yew hedge. Yew grows more rapidly than is often imagined. It is dense and easy to maintain, provides a dark background to highlight the colour of the flowers in the foreground and is the plant of choice for formal hedging in many British and European gardens. The planting within the gardens is not always traditional, but the yew hedging certainly is.

An Edible Forest Garden was added in 2011 to illustrate an alternative approach to food production. Modelled on the storeys of growth you find in a young woodland, it works up from perennial vegetables at ground level to herbs, fruiting shrubs and nut trees intertwined with vines. This system is easily maintained once established, highly productive and can be adapted to almost any size of garden. Planted here are six different sorts of *Prunus avium* (mazzard or wild cherry), once cultivated as a food crop in the area, and *Mahonia* x *media* 'Lionel Fortescue', a winter-flowering barberry raised in Devon that surprisingly has edible fruit.

Although space allows different areas of the garden to peak at different seasons, every plant and feature still has to excel, and Rosemoor is constantly being critiqued by the curator and gardeners. The original plan for the Queen Mother's Rose Garden had positioned spring-flowering Japanese cherries in each corner. These have since been replaced by *Philadelphus* 'Virginal' and variegated pittosporums, which combine more effectively with the roses when in flower. More recently, it was decided that a shady, winding path leading from the Rock Gully towards Lady Anne's Garden was in need of livening up and a member of staff suggested a stumpery. Jagged tree stumps transported from Rosemoor's woodlands were turned upside-down all along the 91-metre/300-foot path, overlapping and connecting to form a sculptural setting for rare ferns and shade-loving plants. Completed in autumn 2017, this atmospheric new feature fits well with Lady Anne's gardening ethos and use of choice plants.

Rosemoor has developed a speciality in seasonal pots. These are dotted strategically around the garden, making use of 40,000

'Although space allows different areas of the garden to peak at different seasons, every plant and feature still has to excel, and Rosemoor is constantly being critiqued by the curator and gardeners.'

The Queen Mother's Rose Garden is awash with colour and fragrance when in full bloom, and an all-round sensory experience for visitors.

The Foliage Garden in late summer at RHS Garden Rosemoor features striking plants like *Phormium tenax* 'All Black', *Miscanthus sinensis* 'Rotsilber' and the rounded hummocks of *Euphorbia*, showing how plants make an architectural impact in sun or shade.

Left: The rustic gateway leading to the Fruit and Vegetable Garden is decorated with blossom in spring and fruit in autumn.

Below: The Fruit and Vegetable Garden at RHS Garden Rosemoor is full of 'take home' ideas with its raised beds, geometrically planted salads and 'step-over' fruit trees.

Bottom: Shrub roses in their abundant glory weave romance and nostalgia into a summertime visit.

Right: Borage and other herbs add flowers and fragrance to the potager, where edible crops are also used as ornamentals. A dual purpose role that is ideal in a small garden.

bulbs to brighten dark corners in winter. From spring to autumn the pots are filled with bedding produced in the garden's nursery and placed where people are likely to linger. By the thatched shelter in the Cottage Garden, dainty *Fuchsia* 'Dying Embers' follows on from daffodils and tulips.

Changes to the garden follow a rolling three-year plan. Elizabeth Banks always believed that the formal garden rooms should evolve; and some have already been renovated twice. In 2019 a new Cool Garden in pastel shades will replace the former Spiral Garden. Award-winning designer Jo Thompson has made use of blue and white flowers to contrast with the iconic Hot Garden nearby, incorporating water features and showing how permeable surfaces can help deal with heavy rainfall.

Rosemoor strives to showcase the best of horticulture and constantly improve its range of plants, making each garden area distinctive. The woodland above Lady Anne's Garden, which offers sheltered, well-drained conditions, is now home to an expanding collection of plants from the regions of the world which were once part of Gondwana, the southern supercontinent that broke up about 180 million years ago.

A woodland estate of 40.5 hectares/100 acres surrounds the garden and has been gradually transformed since 2005. Conifers originally planted for timber are being replaced to favour the growth of native broadleaved species, predominantly oak, for future generations to enjoy. Local schoolchildren have helped by planting native trees and shrubs at River Wood, a 5.3-hectare/12-acre strip of land bordering the River Torridge, as well as English bluebell bulbs beneath beech trees to the east of the arboretum. Swathes of yellow-

flowered *Rhododendron luteum* will form a transition from the garden to the bluebell woods, resulting in a springtime attraction when both are in flower.

In addition to everything Rosemoor offers as a garden, it runs a packed calendar of over a hundred events a year, including a Rose Weekend and Apple Festival. This has dramatically increased visitor numbers despite being over an hour from the nearest motorway. The first ever Rosemoor Flower Show, held in August 2017, attracted 9,000 people over three days. The RHS National Rhododendron Show and Competition, now in its tenth year, attracts entries from the great Cornish gardens, as well as Exbury and Savill gardens, and is gaining in popularity. Rosemoor has further broadened its appeal as a venue by hosting weddings and the Real Ale, Gin and Music Fest, as well as antiques weekends and magic shows for families. The Garden Room, a dedicated events building, has recently been completed next to the restaurant. Diversifying in this way has introduced the garden to a new and varied audience, also boosting the local economy. Once visitors discover the garden, many return to enjoy it at other times of the year.

Rosemoor rejoices in its freedom from convention, particularly the ability to grow plants not normally associated with the south west of Britain. First there were roses. Soon alpines will make an appearance, in troughs, pots, raised beds and a new display glasshouse. In the light of previous successes, this is sure to impress.

After trimming the lawn edges on the Trials Field at Wisley to keep it tidy, the next job to do is to rake up the grass.

# Behind the scenes

# Behind the scenes

The big oak door of the Laboratory at RHS Garden Wisley is the kind of door you normally wouldn't dare enter. If you have ever been to Wisley, you are likely to have walked past it on your way from the main entrance into the garden and may have wondered why it is so forbidding. Step inside, through a second door, and you feel you are entering a dark inner sanctum, with the names of past directors and other plaques on the oak-panelled walls. For just over one hundred years this building has been home to the laboratories, the herbarium and the advisory team.

The building was designed to suit the requirements of horticultural researchers a long time ago, and circumstances have changed. Scientists are facing greater challenges than ever before, with biosecurity top of the agenda: we all need to help prevent potentially devastating pests and diseases from entering the UK. In preparation for the extreme weather events likely to increase due to the changing climate, research is also needed on ways to make gardens more resilient to drought and rain. The vital research of Wisley's world-leading horticultural scientists will advance further thanks to the improved facilities of the National Centre for Horticultural Science and Learning, due to open at Wisley in 2020.

In the future, we are likely to see and hear even more of what the RHS is busily doing behind the scenes to help people get the most from their gardens and growing spaces. The advisory service strives to provide RHS members and all interested parties with authoritative guidance based on the latest scientific evidence, and gives them the means to make informed choices about how they garden. RHS specialists in the naming of cultivated plants will continue to be of benefit to gardeners and scientists worldwide, ensuring that our knowledge and enjoyment of plants rests on a stable system. Essential to this work is the herbarium, which serves a truly remarkable number of uses. The RHS also plays a major role in the international registration of new plant varieties, with responsibility for nine plant groups. The society's plant health scientists focus on the identification, management and control of pests and diseases that widely affect garden plants, from the dreaded honey fungus to the relentless problem of slugs. The sheer range of research projects that the RHS undertakes (often in collaboration with other institutes or universities) might surprise. Current fields of interest include the genetic code of daffodils, the society's lost herbarium and the effect of front gardens on wellbeing.

RHS volunteers rarely receive enough recognition and most people are unaware of the scale of their contribution, but without their input in critical areas the society would be unable to deliver the service that it does today. Volunteers, with their expertise and enthusiasm, are ever-present in the most unexpected places. Sometimes they lay the foundations; at other times they add a touch of finesse. The charitable work of the RHS can go further because of them, and for that they deserve our thanks.

Left: RHS Chief Horticulturist Guy Barter, a scientist and experienced practical gardener, helps with a visitor's enquiry at an RHS show.

Right: The advisory team keeps up to date with information on problems like horse chestnut leaf-mining moth, first identified in Wimbledon in 2002.

# Ask the experts

## GARDENING ADVICE

There has always been an enquiry service to assist RHS members with their gardening problems. In the early days, members would often send handwritten letters addressed to the director of horticulture for forwarding to whoever could best respond. A director's report from the 1920s notes that wisteria was a common subject of enquiry, but that too little detail was sent to make a firm comment in many cases. In time, a single adviser was employed, who relied on personal expertise and information stored in a card-indexing system. Then the RHS became a much bigger membership organisation, and in 1995 the service expanded. By 2007 there were eight advisers dealing with 55,000 enquiries a year. Today there are the equivalent of eleven dealing with over 105,000. Around 25,000 enquiries are fielded at RHS flower shows (where anyone can ask for gardening advice, including visitors, exhibitors and judges).

What these figures do not reveal is how the advisory service functions as the motor of an 'advice cycle'. All questions are recorded and used as significant data. This allows the society to keep in touch with gardeners' current concerns and to pick up on any new problems. In response, appropriate advice can quickly be shared with the public online. The advisory service is also connected up to other branches of RHS work – for example, by supporting colleagues involved in community outreach projects, or by suggesting ideas to illustrate in RHS gardens (such as Wisley's trial of alternatives to box hedging). Perhaps most important is the reciprocal link with science: advice is authoritative because it is grounded in evidence derived from RHS scientific expertise; equally, information received through the advisory service suggests new lines of investigation.

Over the years, the RHS has built up a wealth of guidance based on topics dealt with by advisers. All this information is available to members and non-members alike on the RHS website – more than 1,200 pages of advice and plant information, receiving around 30 million hits annually at the last count. The RHS weekly question-and-answer session on Twitter provides a taster of the members' advisory service, and experts are often on hand during special events at RHS gardens, such as fruit-naming days.

Gardening is such a vast subject that questions can veer from the legal implications of high hedges to the identity of a rare alpine. The majority of enquiries, though, are about growing, pruning and propagating plants. Woody plants, which are slow to grow, expensive to replace and essential to a garden's structure, take up by far the greatest part of advisory work. Apples, roses and acers frequently come up. A fair proportion of enquiries concern vegetables, but there are surprisingly few on lawns. Other topics vary in popularity over time. Houseplants, although currently fashionable, figure less, possibly because people treat them as expendable. Scientific enquiries, such as pollution-filtering hedges for school playgrounds, are on the rise. Advisers handle all general and horticultural matters, but sometimes specialist knowledge from the library, herbarium, science department or gardens is needed.

Weather-related queries are common, and it is possible to identify weather conditions such as late frosts from the type of enquiries received; people tend not to notice the damage initially but over the following three to six weeks dozens of enquiries come in. A memorable year was 2011, when the advisory team received

200 enquiries about cordylines affected by the cold weather in the previous December. As well as the crown of leaves being damaged by frost, the stems oozed a smelly liquid indicating bacterial infection. Staff rapidly identified this as a new problem and were able to alert the public. In 2018 the main concern was drought and how to use water wisely. Many people contacted the service about plants dying (even young trees that had been in the ground for several years) and runner beans not cropping (due to the hot weather).

Troublesome pests and diseases are another constant source of concern. About 20,000 enquiries on this subject are received every year (representing just under a third of all logged enquiries and roughly the same quantity as weather-related ones). Of these, 10,000 require specialist knowledge and are handled by scientists. Honey fungus has headed up the annually published top-ten list of diseases for twenty-two years running, ever since rankings began. In wet years, slugs and snails invariably come first among pests.

Through member enquiries, the RHS is often first to receive reports of pests and diseases new to Britain, some of which prove to be more damaging than others. Between three and five new records are logged annually. Since the year 2000 this has included horse chestnut leaf-mining moth (2002), fuchsia gall mite (2007), sempervivum leaf-miner (2008) and kerria twig and leaf blight (2014). It is possible to follow the spread of problems according to the location of enquiries. Fuchsia gall mite (first discovered in Brazil in the late 1970s) has been tracked heading towards London from the south coast, allowing the RHS to take a more proactive approach in warning gardeners of its approach. With the help of citizen science (see pages 212–13), the RHS is currently monitoring rosemary beetle, lily beetle, berberis sawfly, box tree moth and hemerocallis gall midge.

RHS entomologists hold records dating back many decades, an invaluable resource. This data has been used to create animated maps of the changing distribution of several pests, supplemented by more recent sightings sent in by the general public through citizen science surveys. Lily beetle, which started as a single red dot in 1939, is shown to cover most of England by 2015. In a new initiative prompted by the elevated risks to plant health (see pages 108–11), the RHS advisory service is inviting anyone in the UK who finds an exotic pest or disease in their garden to get in touch. It could make all the difference.

Below: Honey fungus has long been a problem in gardens and, although much is known about its habits, there is still plenty more to discover. Gardeners can have instant access to details about its lifecycle and control by clicking on the RHS website.

Right, clockwise from top: When pruning, remove crossing stems to avoid rubbing and entry of fungal diseases; control aphids when populations are small; box tree moth has been the top pest on the list at the RHS in previous years; lily beetle is easy to spot – both adults and larvae cause damage.

Left: Close scrutiny of specimens through a microscope allows researchers to analyse problems in great detail.

Right: A scientist at work at Wisley on the 'Sustainable Resource Use in Horticulture' project plots, with the aim of discovering how viburnums respond to different growing media.

# Under the microscope

### SCIENTIFIC RESEARCH

Science has been important to the RHS since its foundation and today it underpins all the society does. Over the decades, RHS scientists have contributed to many important studies, particularly on pests and diseases. James Kirkham Ramsbottom (1891–1925), an unsung hero, discovered that heat treatment was effective against narcissus eelworm, thereby saving the British daffodil industry from disaster. In the 1920s, George Fox Wilson, the RHS's first full-time entomologist, pioneered a biological control for glasshouse whitefly using a parasitic wasp. It was replaced some years later by a more effective species, *Encarsia formosa*, and the RHS remained the only supplier of it for the amateur gardener in the UK until the 1940s. The groundbreaking botanist E.K. Janaki Ammal joined RHS staff in 1945, just after co-authoring the monumental *Chromosome Atlas of Cultivated Plants*, and pursued her work on genetic inheritance in the society's laboratories until 1951.

More recently, research has focused on slugs, honey fungus, box blight and box tree caterpillar, all difficult problems for gardeners. Today's scientific team numbers up to eighty staff and PhD students, of whom twenty are research scientists. Their work flows from the four broad themes of the RHS science strategy: a global knowledge bank for gardening and garden plants; plant health in gardens; gardening in a changing world; and plant science for all (people, plants and planet). In the long term, the RHS aims to become the pre-eminent institution for horticultural science, and the new National Centre for Horticultural Science and Learning at RHS Garden Wisley is a step in that direction.

Research is carried out in a multitude of ways, either directly by departmental staff, through commission or sponsorship, or jointly with universities and other research institutes. In 2018, for example, the RHS ran a study in partnership with the Royal Holloway, London, into the pests and diseases most affecting Britain's gardens. With colleagues from the University of Reading, the science team has also recently succeeded in mapping part of the genetic code of the daffodil *Narcissus poeticus*, opening the way towards a test that can distinguish different varieties from their dormant bulbs.

Reviews of published evidence on topics important to gardeners are also undertaken, so that people can take advantage of practical solutions and make informed choices. A wide-ranging report on the benefits of gardens in towns and cities led to the current Greening Grey Britain campaign (see pages 70–73) and has been followed up with ongoing research into how green roofs, garden hedges and other forms of urban greening can moderate air temperature, retain rainfall and trap aerial pollutants. In 2016 a report on sustainable growing media asked why novel materials had not replaced peat more widely and suggested ways for researchers to improve progress. Most recently, the second of two influential reports on climate change is setting the agenda for future projects (see page 106).

The results of RHS research are shared through numerous channels, including Britain in Bloom, the RHS Campaign for School Gardening, and the network of affiliated societies, as well as through displays at RHS gardens and flower shows. Information is also made available through publications and the website's popular advisory and plant selector pages. The latest RHS advice on what best to plant in a wildlife garden, along with the related Plants for Pollinators initiative, incorporates the outcomes of a four-year study completed

in 2013. This project used experimental plots at Wisley to test whether insects prefer native plants. The message for gardeners is that the more flowers a garden can offer throughout the year, the more bees, hoverflies and pollinating insects it will attract. A densely growing planting scheme will also support more plant-dwelling insects.

The RHS has made a pledge to develop research skills in horticultural science by investing in post-graduate research. The number of PhD students being supervised by RHS scientists has risen in the last five years from an average of three to ten, all concentrating on topics ultimately of benefit to gardeners and the horticultural industry. An area clearly in need of further investigation is slug control. No one has yet discovered a definitive solution to this problem, yet it is high on the RHS top ten list of pests. A PhD study is currently identifying precisely which slug or gastropod species are found in UK gardens, while another is assessing a range of nematodes as biocontrol agents.

Other projects work towards solutions for potential problems that could have damaging consequences in the future, so that growers can be prepared. This includes the risk management associated with *Xylella fastidiosa*, a dangerous bacterial plant disease causing concern in mainland Europe; and rose rosette virus, a serious threat in the United States, with huge implications for the rose industry if it entered Britain.

While plant health remains a priority, research covers a great diversity of topics. One study is finding the best flavoured rosemary for commercial use by looking at factors such as cultivar choice and environment. Others are investigating the effect of plants on indoor air quality and the likely impact of invasive plants due to climate change in the UK. Questions of soil science are being addressed and an innovative experiment measuring the effect of front gardens on health and wellbeing is underway in Salford.

In view of developments at the RHS, this is an exciting time for horticultural science. There is the prospect of getting to the bottom of questions that have never been thoroughly explored before, as well as of anticipating challenges on the horizon. Thomas Andrew Knight, considered the father of horticultural science, and influential in the early days of the society, was convinced that scientific enquiry could yield techniques and practices that make sense for gardeners. He would surely be delighted to see the present level of activity, and to know that an even more productive phase is about to begin.

A scientist compares moths in the Entomology Laboratory at Wisley.

# Climate change

Our changing climate will affect the way we garden and what we grow. In time, it may even change what gardens mean to us. According to an RHS survey, the majority of UK gardeners are willing to adapt but would feel better prepared if they had access to more practical information. Understandably, people have concerns and questions. What types of tree can be planted now and yet thrive through the changing climate in decades to come? Will pests and diseases spread more quickly? Will lawns need to be replaced?

The survey was part of a detailed study carried out in partnership with the universities of Sheffield and Reading. The results were presented in 2017 in an 80-page report entitled *Gardening in a Changing Climate* and an accompanying 12-page summary. An earlier report, *Gardening in the Global Greenhouse*, had been completed in 2002, when scientific predictions suggested a Mediterranean-type climate for the UK. Over the last fifteen years, climate models have evolved and incorporated recent data. Analysis now points to more variable climatic conditions marked by extremes of prolonged drought and heavy rainstorms. Average temperature is still projected to increase in all seasons across the UK, and much of the country could be frost-free by 2100, but the south is likely to experience drier summers than the north, which will be facing wetter winters. Specific growing conditions will depend on local geography. In some areas, gardeners will need to choose heat-tolerant plants and capture rainfall for use in dry periods; in others, raised beds could be used to lift plants clear of the water table.

One way the RHS can help gardeners meet the challenges of climate change is by providing the best possible advice, both in print and online, as well as at shows, and through campaigns and public events. In 2018, talks on *Gardening in a Changing Climate* were held jointly by the RHS and the Royal Meteorological Society in Manchester, Bristol and Birmingham. RHS gardens provide living examples, such as Hyde Hall's experimental Dry Garden and the rainfall features of Rosemoor's forthcoming Cool Garden. Climate change also sets priorities for research, so that advice remains up to date. In collaboration with Cranfield University, the RHS has appointed the UK's first water scientist with a focus on domestic gardening, tasked with researching innovative, cost-effective technologies to deal with too much or too little water.

Gardens could in future mitigate some effects of climate change and bring wider benefits to society. The 2017 report highlighted what gardeners can do to help capture carbon, shelter wildlife, support pollinating insects, moderate local temperature and alleviate flash flooding. It also pointed to the upside of a longer growing season and the possibility of new plant selections with greater resilience. As we gain a clearer picture of the impacts of climate change, the RHS is helping prepare gardeners for the challenges and opportunities to come so that we can all keep gardening successfully.

Below: The RHS demonstrated how to garden in a changing climate with this mixed planting of *Aeonium* 'Zwartkop', grasses and pansies in their 'Garden for a Changing Climate' at Chatsworth Flower Show in 2017, designed by Andy Clayden and Dr Ross Cameron.

Bottom: The 'Futureproof Waterproof Landscape Garden' at RHS Tatton Flower Show in 2011 proved that climate change will not stop us creating beautiful gardens. We just need to adapt our idea of what is beautiful.

Right: There are hundreds of ideas for drought-tolerant plants in the Dry Garden at RHS Hyde Hall, with plenty more to be added every year.

Left: An olive tree infected by the dreaded bacterium *Xylella fastidiosa*.

Right: Box tree moth (*Cydalima perspectalis*) is beautiful, but destructive in the UK and no friend of the gardener.

# Keeping gardens safe

### PLANT HEALTH

Global trade means that a greater volume and diversity of plants and plant-based products are being imported to the UK than ever before. They arrive from a larger number of destinations and travel more quickly than in the past. The result is an unprecedented risk of new pests and diseases entering the country and becoming established. Evidence points to an increasing number of outbreaks. More than 1,000 pests and diseases are flagged as potential threats on the government's UK Plant Health Risk Register, some of which could irretrievably change our natural and garden landscapes if introduced. Of greatest concern is the bacterium *Xylella fastidiosa*, capable of infecting more than 350 different plant species. Native to the Americas, where it affects citrus, grapevines and other crops, it was confirmed in Europe in 2013. High-risk plants include olive and cherry trees, rosemary, lavender and hebe.

Faced with this rapidly evolving situation, the RHS is making plant health a priority on several levels: advice for gardeners, best practice in its own gardens and shows, research into methods of control and management, and a concerted approach with other organisations to provide policymakers with relevant information. The RHS has accumulated decades of scientific expertise and it is more important than ever for it to pursue its work on the monitoring, detection and identification of pests and diseases. An internal Plant Health Working Group helps coordinate a joined-up approach across the society, and the RHS is collaborating with external groups such as Defra (including the Plant Health and Seed Inspectorate), Fera Science and the Horticultural Trades Association.

The RHS is the only organisation in Britain conducting surveillance for garden pests and diseases. It does this through its advisory service (see pages 98–101), which receives approximately 10,000 specialist enquiries on pests and diseases annually, as well as through research work. As a result, the RHS is often first to identify pests and diseases new to Britain. Some of these establish quickly while others do not spread widely, at least initially, but it is important to map and monitor them so that action can be taken in time if the situation changes. Lily beetle has been in the UK since 1939 but began spreading rapidly only from the 1990s. Along with box blight, it is one of the most damaging problems to affect gardens in the last couple of decades, while emerging threats include box tree caterpillars, fuchsia gall mite and *Phytophthora*. Ash dieback, a lethal fungal disease of ash trees, was detected in the UK in 2012 and its full impact is as yet unknown.

In a two-sided approach, the RHS is taking action to minimise the risk of spreading new or harmful pests and diseases through its activities, while also protecting the health of its own plant collections. For this reason, the plant species most likely to be infected with *Xylella fastidiosa* are no longer permitted at RHS flower shows unless grown in the UK. In addition, judges will now consider the health of plants when assessing show gardens. The RHS is stepping up vigilance in its own gardens and plant centres, and will source UK-grown plant material where possible. Developing a list of approved suppliers may help with this. Any imported semi-mature trees will be kept in quarantine for at least twelve months. Plant health has been a factor in planning the developments at RHS Garden Wisley, where the new Welcome

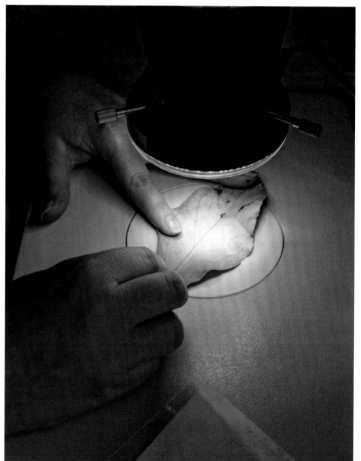

> 'The RHS has accumulated decades of scientific expertise and it is more important than ever for it to pursue its work on the monitoring, detection and identification of pests and diseases.'

Building will incorporate an advice desk: limiting enquiries to the front entrance is a precaution. Any samples taken in for analysis will then be bagged and transferred to the laboratories in the National Centre for Horticultural Science and Learning.

Because the stakes are high, plant health needs to be everyone's responsibility, including home gardeners. Changing our habits and making different choices can have a huge impact. High on the list is not bringing cuttings or plants back from holiday. An RHS survey in 2018 found that this is common practice when returning from Europe, and is possibly how fuchsia gall mite entered the UK (now widespread in the south-east). Another positive step is to enquire where plants were produced before buying from nurseries and to check the plants for signs of problems. Where possible, favour stock grown in the UK, or even propagate your own. And ideally, keep

any new plants in isolation for a few weeks when you get them home, or at least monitor them closely after planting. Anyone can contribute to the collective effort of surveillance by reporting new sightings of target pests and diseases to Defra or the RHS.

As well as keeping the public informed, the RHS is urging policymakers and the horticultural industry to take further action. At the Chelsea Flower Show in 2018, RHS President Sir Nicholas Bacon spoke about the society's responsibility towards biosecurity, saying: 'the industry is looking at the issue in a piecemeal way. We hope to provide a consolidation of effort.' This could include introducing a plant health certification scheme and making the existing plant health insurance scheme mandatory, with tighter controls to ensure every supplier reaches a minimum standard. The RHS is also calling on the government to set up a cross-sector governance group, modelled on the New Zealand example, and to reinforce regulations and border controls for plant material in personal baggage.

While it is not possible to predict what future problems will emerge, it is important to take precautions now and stay vigilant. Above all, efforts need to be focused on preventing *Xylella fastidiosa* from entering the UK supply chain. The RHS is doing all it can to help. Gardeners can do their bit too.

Left, clockwise from top: A scientist conducting research into agapanthus gall midge at the Field Research Facility, Wisley; pests can be found on all parts of a plant; sometimes scientists grow samples in petri dishes to help them accurately identify problems; testing for *Phytophthora* root rot, a vexing problem for gardeners.

Right, top: Often it is useful to grow plants for experiments in the controlled conditions of a laboratory.

Right, bottom: Rhododendron roots with suspected *Phytophthora* root rot.

Below: When identifying a pest or problem, it is always easier if you see the patient.

Left: Positioning a ColorChecker while digitising a herbarium specimen. This allows scientists to compare the colour of the specimen with the consistent colour on the chequerboard.

Right: Herbarium specimens are not only of scientific interest, they are often works of art.

# Cut and dried

## HERBARIUM

There is something fascinatingly mysterious about a herbarium if you don't happen to work in one, but the basic idea is quite simple. A herbarium is a collection of dried, pressed plants mounted on sheets of card that can be consulted year-round, at times when living plants are not in flower, fruit or leaf. The specimens include notes of where and when they were collected. They are stored in flat folders in banks of cupboards arranged in a logical sequence, and are used by botanists for the identification and classification of plants.

Most herbaria contain wild plants, but the RHS herbarium at Wisley is dedicated to garden plants. It holds 86,000 pressed specimens, supplemented by over 35,000 photographic slides, 8,000 prints and 3,500 paintings. There are also around 13,000 pages of plant collectors' notes and a large quantity of fruits, seeds and samples of wood or bark. The oldest specimen is of *Lavandula* x *intermedia*, dating from 1731. Other treasures include a potato plant found by Charles Darwin in the Chonos Archipelago, off the southern coast of Chile, and 1,000 items collected in China by the great explorer George Forrest.

For several decades from around 1820, the RHS sponsored plant collecting trips around the world, having decided that not enough material returning on ships survived the perilous journey. They received not only living plants but also pressed specimens, primarily for identification and naming. The society's plant collectors included David Douglas (collecting in North America), Robert Fortune (China) and Carl Theodor Hartweg (North, Central and South America). In 1856 the original herbarium collections were sold at auction, in part to relieve the society's debts. Recent research has revealed where

the specimens now reside, and these include the major herbaria in Switzerland, France, Sweden and London.

A second herbarium was begun in 1903. Based on the collection of Revd George Henslow (RHS professor of botany 1880–1918), it was expanded by the society's own collectors from 1917 but only found its current focus following the first edition of the *International Code of Nomenclature for Cultivated Plants* in 1953. Botanist Chris Brickell, who later became director of the RHS, decided at this point that the herbarium should specialise in cultivated plants; it is now one of the leading herbaria of this kind in the world, and the largest in Britain. For more than fifty years, staff and volunteers have been collecting, pressing and photographing plants from RHS gardens, trials and shows, as well as cultivars submitted by plant breeders for registration (see pages 116–19). They have helped assemble comprehensive collections of the most important garden ornamentals, ranging from *Abelia* through to *Zosima*. The herbaria of the British Pteridological Society (cultivated ferns) and Alpine Garden Society are also housed at Wisley.

Certain specimens have a special significance because they help fix the names of cultivars. Designated as nomenclatural standards, they provide the definitive name and description reference of a plant with which others can be compared. The herbarium holds 5,000 of these and is actively acquiring more. Paintings of award-winning plants and photographs can also become nomenclatural standards for a cultivar name. Some, like *Delphinium* 'Nymph', exhibited by Pritchard & Sons in July 1922, are the only remaining records of long-lost cultivars. *Chrysanthemum* 'Desert Song' was thought to have died out some time after the 1950s, until an RHS member asked for help in identifying a

plant growing in their greenhouse. The enquiry, received in November 2008, led staff to a painting of 'Desert Song' held by the herbarium, and it was a perfect match.

The herbarium is open to anyone wishing to consult the collections, such as students, researchers and RHS members. Plant Heritage National Collection holders visit to receive advice on the preparation and archiving of their own specimens, to trace old varieties or check that their plants are correctly named. Even students of fashion and design come in search of inspiration. However, for information to be more easily accessible to a wider audience, both in the UK and internationally, all specimens will eventually be digitised and made freely available on the RHS website. Wisley's new National Centre for Horticultural Science and Learning will include a digitisation suite for this purpose.

Pressed plants in the herbarium and living plants in RHS gardens are catalogued on the same database, creating a joint source of reference with total agreement in naming. This same horticultural database is used to produce *The RHS Plant Finder* (the 2018 edition of which contained 76,000 plant names, all checked for accuracy by RHS botanists). The RHS also contributes to the *International Code of Nomenclature for Cultivated Plants*, which ensures consistent and correct naming of plants worldwide. Related publications include the *RHS Colour Chart*, developed for consistency in comparing colours and now a standard reference. The 920 shades are compared with living plant material and noted to provide an accurate record of colour. This is important because colours fade when a specimen is pressed. Although designed for plants, the chart has also been adopted in the food, cosmetic, pharmaceutical and fashion industries.

Among its many uses, the herbarium serves as a resource for scientific work and also as a historical record. Herbarium staff have made a study of invasive plants like giant hogweed (*Heracleum mantegazzianum*), using data from herbarium specimens to help trace their introduction and distribution throughout Britain. Another example would be a scientist looking at how plants with hairy leaves can trap particulates from the air; by leafing through the specimens of a suitable subject, like *Stachys byzantina*, they could establish which cultivars are most likely to have the required characteristics.

When the herbarium moves to its new location in Wisley's science centre it will offer better facilities for consultation and secure the collections for perpetuity in an environmentally controlled store. Equally important, visitors will have views into working areas for the first time. The rich and wonderful world of the RHS herbarium will come out from behind the scenes.

Left: A herbarium specimen of *Delphinium* 'David Mannion', collected in July 2001, was made from a plant that was trialled at RHS Garden Wisley, having been raised, introduced and submitted by Ken Harbutt of Rougham Hall Nurseries.

Above: Comparing the tones on a colour chart with a dahlia specimen in the herbarium.

Right: Painting of *Delphinium* 'Nymph' by Elsie Katherine Kohnlein, one of many talented botanical artists employed over the decades by the RHS.

Below: The herbarium is used to check plants for specific uses. The hairy leaves of *Stachys byzantina* 'Silver Carpet' filter polluting particulates from the air.

# It started with daffodils ...

## PLANT REGISTRATION

Certain groups of plants, like daffodils, lilies and rhododendrons, have captured the imagination of gardeners. Due to the length of time they have been in cultivation and the extensive breeding carried out to achieve different traits, names have been duplicated and the origins of plants lost. To ensure consistency of naming and avoid confusion, it is essential that their correct identities are recorded. Pressed specimens of cultivated plants that are known to be true to type are preserved in the herbarium at RHS Garden Wisley (see pages 112–15), and the RHS maintains registers and checklists that document a plant's name, its parents, origin, description and date of introduction. This painstaking work is part of a worldwide endeavour for the benefit of everyone who works with and enjoys garden plants.

Official cultivar registration came into being in 1952, intended ultimately as a means to record the cultivar names of all plants in cultivation. This is achieved through the various International Cultivar Registration Authorities (ICRA), which are appointed by the International Society for Horticultural Science and given responsibility for a specific plant group. The ICRA network is spread across many countries, including the United States, China, India and South Africa, and at present covers seventy-seven plant groups. The RHS takes care of nine – daffodils, delphiniums, rhododendrons, lilies, orchids, dahlias, *Dianthus* (carnations and pinks), conifers and clematis – and processes well over 3,000 new names a year, ensuring that they conform to the *International Code of Nomenclature for Cultivated Plants* and that none are used twice. An ICRA does not, however, rule on the distinctiveness or value of new cultivars, and the process is voluntary, relying on the cooperation of breeders to register their plants.

The RHS handles the official registration of more groups of plants than any other individual organisation in the world, and it has occupied this special position since the mid-1960s. The reasons for this are historical, because from the late nineteenth century the RHS was already helping to put in place processes to list cultivar names and hybrids, in particular of daffodils and orchids, and thus had built up decades of experience in compiling checklists before the official system was formalised in 1952. The quality of today's registers rests on the contribution of certain dedicated individuals, both in the past and the present day.

The origin of plant registration can be traced back to the work of Peter Barr (1826–1909), a bulb and seed merchant who had a shop in Covent Garden and was passionate about daffodils. In 1884 he was the driving force behind a special conference organised by the RHS. This resulted in what became known as the *Conference Catalogue of Narcissus*, included with which was a list of cultivated varieties. In 1907 the first *Classified List of Daffodil Names* was published (called 'classified' because the cultivar's horticultural classification forms part of the description). A second list, which appeared in 1908, instructed the Narcissus Committee 'to refuse in future to register names which are either so nearly like existing names as to be likely to cause confusion, or such as are foolish, or are phrases and are not names at all'. In much the same spirit, the most recent edition of the official *Classified List and Register of Daffodils* was published in 2008 and contains just under 30,000 names.

Orchids, renowned for the complexity of naming and parentage, were soon generating as much discussion as daffodils. A conference on

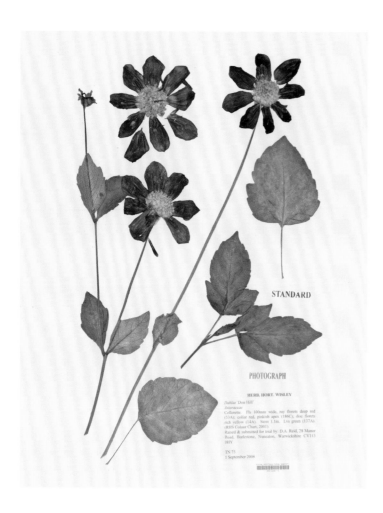

STANDARD

PHOTOGRAPH

HERB. HORT. WISLEY

*Dahlia* 'Don Hill'
*Asteraceae*
Collarette Fls 100mm wide, ray florets deep red
(53A), collar red, pinkish apex (186C), disc florets
rich yellow (14A). Stem 1.1m. Lvs green (137A).
(RHS Colour Chart, 2001)
Raised & submitted for trial by: D.A. Reid, 28 Manor
Road, Barlestone, Nuneaton, Warwickshire CV13
0HY

TN 75
1 September 2006

their nomenclature took place in Liverpool in 1886 and was attended by leading orchidologist Heinrich Gustav Reichenbach. When the first bigeneric orchid hybrid had appeared in 1883 and was named *Aceras-herminium* by combining the names of both parents, it was clear that future naming was likely to be contentious unless rules were established. The appearance of hybrids involving several orchid genera made their naming even more problematic. The current register for orchids in fact started with a system established in 1895 by the firm of Sander & Sons, which, in 1906, issued the first *Sander's List of Orchid Hybrids*. The RHS took up the baton in 1960, was later appointed the ICRA for orchids, and has ever since produced three-yearly volumes of new orchid hybrids, or grexes as they are correctly known. The latest, published in 2017, lists over 9,000, and the total number of grexes registered by the end of 2018 came to more than 173,000.

In the early twentieth century, the RHS was involved in compiling checklists for various other plant groups, including the *Tentative Check-list of Delphinium Names* in 1949. Although the RHS became the ICRA for most of these groups, registration of some passed to other organisations: tulips to the Dutch Royal General Bulb Growers' Association (KAVB), for example, and camellias to the International Camellia Society, based at the Kunming Botanic Garden in China.

Many early lists concentrated exclusively on varieties in cultivation, omitting any that had disappeared from commerce; but a great shift of emphasis took place thanks to carnation enthusiast and horticultural historian Audrey Robinson. The *First International Dianthus Regsiter* appeared in 1974 and, although it contained more than 3,000 names, it did not include many old cultivars known to survive in private collections. Audrey wanted the register to be more comprehensive and undertook much of the task of recording all known names of dianthus cultivars produced over the centuries. As a result, the 1983 edition included 27,000 names and became an indispensable historical guide for the gardener and grower. The third edition, published by the RHS in 2017, contains over 44,000 names. The expansion is due to extensive research by botanist and long-serving RHS registrar Alan Leslie, and particularly to his success in obtaining a large number of records from Japan, where, surprisingly perhaps, plant breeders are keen on *Dianthus*.

Since the 1990s, most registers have been held in the form of databases, making it easier to produce the printed registers and the registration supplements published every year. Two RHS registers (on daffodils and orchids) can now be consulted online through the RHS website, and in July 2018 the RHS launched an online system for registering new orchid hybrids. A Brazilian hybrid was registered on the day of the launch, since when about a quarter of new orchid registrations have come by this route. A registration site for dahlias and daffodils will soon follow, delivering a much better experience for registrants and encouraging more people to register their new plants for the sake of nomenclatural stability.

# Helping hands

### VOLUNTEERS

There is no doubt that the RHS can aim higher and achieve more thanks to the support of its volunteers – over 2,000 in all – who generously contribute their time, energy and enthusiasm to making so many of the society's activities a success. This includes 1,300 on-site volunteers at gardens and shows; 250 off-site, helping in communities and schools, or acting as mentors and judges; and 700 governance volunteers who perform essential behind-the-scenes functions as members of the RHS Council, plant committees, show judging panels and trials forums. In fact, the number of volunteers has risen to far outrank the society's 970 employees.

As an indication of the force for action that volunteers represent, more than 500 people offered to get involved at RHS Garden Bridgewater, the society's new garden in Salford, in the first year alone. Taking a wider view, the thousands of community groups active in Britain in Bloom and It's Your Neighbourhood (see pages 66–9) work tirelessly year-round to make the places they live in better for people and the environment. These groups come in all shapes and sizes, offering a huge range of volunteer opportunities from *ad hoc* office assistance, to joining regular planting or clean-up days, leading wildlife walks or garden cooking sessions.

On-site volunteers can be found in RHS gardens, at shows, in libraries and laboratories, and even in the office of the RHS magazine, *The Garden*. All five RHS gardens have volunteers giving invaluable hands-on help with garden maintenance. Others prefer to welcome school groups, give guided tours or drive mobility vehicles. Volunteer roles at shows include recruiting new members and helping visitors

find what they are looking for in the floral marquees. Volunteers say they get involved as a way of meeting new people, gaining skills, coping with change or bereavement, or to further a career in horticulture; one of the most frequent reasons given is to support the work of the RHS. Many garden volunteers commit to one day a week year-round and on average stay for six years. Some show volunteers give support at three or more shows during one year, travelling the length and breadth of the UK to help. The RHS is looking to develop more meaningful ways of saying 'thank you' and has launched a long service awards programme, recognising milestones in five-year increments. There are currently thirty volunteers who have been with the RHS for twenty years or longer. The longest serving, Brian Wilson, recently retired after thirty-one years at Harlow Carr.

Although they may not at first sight seem to belong to the same category, the seventeen members of the RHS Council, including the president and treasurer, are also volunteers, and the society could not function without them. They are elected by the society's membership and serve as trustees of the charity. Their role is to set the future direction of the RHS, assess its performance and safeguard its finances. Any major changes must be set before the council, which has the authority to question and challenge all aspects of the society's activities and check that decisions are taken thoughtfully and responsibly. Council members have a range of professional backgrounds and are all highly successful in their field, ensuring that there is a pool of knowledge to assist the society in taking decisions and developing long-term strategies, including the £160-million investment programme. The current council includes garden designers, scientists and horticulturists as well as managers,

bankers and accountants. Potential new members are recruited by the Nominations, Appointments and Governance Committee (one of the six main boards and committees to which the council delegates part of its work), and this body is to some extent responsible for the balance of skills represented. Long gone are the days when council members were by definition the owners of large estates or nurseries, and the council has evolved in recent decades to better reflect the profile of the RHS membership, including the presence of more women. However, there is scope to go further and a keen desire to widen the diversity of the RHS's boards.

The council's Horticulture Board meets four times a year, chaired by the RHS president and attended by members of the society's active tier of specialist committees, who advise on areas such as bursaries, science and education. The meetings are an occasion to report on progress and work collectively on any concerns. Seven of the specialist committees are dedicated to particular plant groups, and five of these have been in existence since the nineteenth century, covering: fruit, vegetables and herbs (the first, since 1858), herbaceous plants, woody plants, bulbs (originally the Daffodil Committee) and orchids. In 1936 rock-garden plants joined the list, followed in 1965 by plants tender in the UK. Each plant committee is composed of plantspeople, renowned growers, scientists, world-class experts and famous names in horticulture who donate their time and expertise voluntarily to the society, ensuring that the committees remain relevant and vibrant. Their combined knowledge and experience is formidable.

Specialist plant committees have various responsibilities. They propose plants for trials, assess plants for RHS awards (including the Award of Garden Merit), judge show exhibits and support RHS initiatives such as Britain in Bloom, Horticulture Matters and Affiliated Societies. The work they do is vital, but not always visible. However, a key part of their remit is outreach, and they are often to be seen at shows, events and RHS Partner Gardens around the country, sharing their knowledge through talks, demonstrations and advice in order to take horticulture to an ever-wider audience.

Members of the specialist plant committees who serve on judging panels at RHS shows help evaluate floral exhibits, trade stands and show gardens for awards. They are looking for plants of excellent quality, superbly displayed with showmanship and flair. Each panel comprises a chairperson, either four or six judges, and a secretary. The judges are volunteer experts from the world of horticulture and design who are independent of the RHS and can draw on a wealth of knowledge. One of the most well-known is Jim Buttress, who, like the judges of a bygone era, still wears a trademark bowler hat. Due to the sheer number and variety of exhibits, there are several judging panels at each show – no less than thirteen at Chelsea, mobilising an incredible seventy-one judges. An RHS medal, particularly Best in Show, can be career-changing, so the utmost care is taken to ensure that the awards received by exhibitors and designers are fair. Each exhibit is judged on its own merits against set criteria rather than against one another, meaning you could in theory have a show where all exhibits achieved a Gold medal standard. The judging process is also overseen by experienced senior judges acting as moderators, who ensure consistency and transparency.

To encourage the best in horticulture, and inspire people to learn more about new and interesting plants, the RHS works with around forty specialist plant societies, including The Alpine Garden Society,

The British Cactus and Succulent Society, The Orchid Society of Great Britain and The National Vegetable Society. Their members are friendly enthusiasts keen to share their enjoyment and knowledge with like-minded gardeners, whether amateur or professional, and improve the understanding, cultivation and conservation of their favourite plants. Plant societies regularly take part in events at RHS gardens. The RHS provides facilities and support for shows, talks, competitions and workshops; and plant society members provide passion, advice and a wide range of interesting plants. Each year RHS Garden Wisley hosts over fifteen events showcasing many well-loved and fascinating groups of plants, including the Conifer Society Show, two British Iris Society shows, a carnivorous plant weekend and the National Dahlia Society Annual Show. In June, the annual Specialist Plant Society Show brings together twenty exhibitors offering fabulous displays and mini masterclasses. Visitors to events at Harlow Carr, Rosemoor and Hyde Hall also benefit from the presence of participating plant societies.

The twelve exceptional and influential individuals who act as RHS ambassadors voluntarily support the society's campaigns and help enrich lives through plants. Television presenter and gardener Alan Titchmarsh, the first appointed, is the figurehead of Horticulture Matters, a campaign to raise the profile of careers in horticulture and fill the 'green skills' gap. Nursery owner and gardening expert Carol Klein joined the scheme as ambassador for RHS Garden Bridgewater. Her grandfather's first job was as a garden boy on the historic estate where the garden is being developed. The youngest representative is George Hassall, from Stalybridge, Greater Manchester, an RHS Young School Gardener of the Year winner. He was just ten years old when

he accepted the role. Like fellow ambassador Jamie Butterworth (who co-founded YoungHort in 2013), he aims to inspire more young people to get involved with gardening.

Volunteers have been part of the RHS since its foundation in 1804. It is a proud tradition, enabling the society to enhance the quality and impact of its work. In order to remain up to date with the needs of volunteers, the RHS is currently reviewing how it can meet the demand for more youth, family and skilled volunteering opportunities, as well as build in more flexibility. In future, it hopes to increase the diversity of volunteers within a more inclusive RHS, improve opportunities for learning and development and, above all, ensure that all volunteers have the best possible experience.

'As an indication of the force for action that volunteers represent, over 500 people offered to get involved at RHS Garden Bridgewater, the society's new garden in Salford, in the first year alone.'

The Upper Pond reflecting the farmhouse at Hyde Hall, with the new Hilltop centre to the left of the photograph. A scene typical of the order and horticultural excellence achieved in all RHS gardens.

# Chapter 7
# Hyde Hall

Left, clockwise from top left: Clover Hill connects the garden to the surrounding landscape; the Dry Garden provides inspiration for anyone gardening in arid conditions; the white flowers of *Viburnum plicatum* f. *plicatum* 'Grandiflorum' in the Serpentine Beds on Clover Hill fade to pink with age; the margins of the Lower Pond provide ample space for *Gunnera manicata* and its vigorous companions; the Dry Garden is used to test plant hardiness – here, *Eryngium bourgatii* 'Picos Blue', acanthus and *Dasylirion wheeleri*; *Cornus sanguinea* 'Midwinter Fire', *Euonymus fortunei*

'Emerald 'n' Gold' and *Erica* in the Winter Garden; the Upper Pond boasts a 'big time' planting of *Gunnera manicata*; (left) the Australia and New Zealand Garden contains plants not often seen in British gardens, and (right) the view across the Dry Garden towards the new Hilltop buildings creates a sense of depth; spikes of *Verbascum* create vertical accents in the Dry Garden.

Right: Tufts of fresh green foliage in spring are the first signs of life in the Robinson Garden, as another gardening season begins.

# Hyde Hall

## ESSEX GARDEN

In 1955, Dr Richard and Helen Robinson moved to Hyde Hall, a timber-framed farmhouse near the small Essex town of South Woodham Ferrers. It had long been a working farm and the land around the house was heaped with rubbish, but this was not the main obstacle to making a garden. It was the location and growing conditions that made its transformation such a remarkable achievement.

Situated on an exposed hill 46 metres/150 feet above sea level and surrounded by flat Essex countryside, the ground bakes hard in summer and freezes in winter. Prevailing winds are south-westerly, but chilling Siberian winds slice through the garden for days on end in winter. The soil, predominantly clay with some gravel pockets, and a pH varying from acidic to alkaline, provides little encouragement. Finally, a statistic that would discourage all but the stout-hearted revealed it to be one of the driest parts of Britain, with an average rainfall of 600 mm/24 inches a year – less than in Jerusalem. Rain in winter makes the soil cold, wet and heavy (although in recent times rainfall has become more erratic, creating different problems).

And so the redoubtable Robinsons began to garden. Clearing the land around the house was arduous and time-consuming, but the scrub was eventually eradicated with the help of pigs. Rubbish was removed and the sticky clay soil improved with vast quantities of manure, mushroom compost and bark. Some sixty young trees bought at auction at nearby Wickford Market were positioned as a framework for the garden. Then the Robinsons got planting, particularly roses, which they knew would like the conditions.

In time, their Herculean efforts gave rise to a garden of themed rooms. A boggy area with varying moisture content became a treat for plant lovers. Known as Hermione's Garden, after actress Hermione Gingold, it was renamed the Robinson Garden in honour of Helen in 2007. In 1968 the Pig Park was absorbed into the garden, planted with hedges and gradually filled with a collection of crab apples (*Malus*), later expanded with the addition of the Malus Field. The early 1970s saw a new rose border and rope walk, with climbing roses and clematis trained on rope swags. Viburnums were introduced, initially in the mixed shrub border, forerunners of Hyde Hall's National Plant Collection of AGM viburnums, which is now dispersed throughout the site. In the late 1970s the Gold Garden was created, inspired by the Golden Garden at Crathes Castle, Scotland.

The Robinsons wanted a woodland with rhododendrons and other ericaceous plants. A shelter belt was planted in 1963 and soil improved to provide suitable conditions, but the project failed because the rhododendrons were rooting into alkaline soil. The Robinsons approached the RHS for advice and the resulting relationship eventually led to Hyde Hall being bequeathed to the RHS: in 1993 the charity inherited a multifaceted garden of 10 hectares/24 acres comprising 6.5 hectares/16 acres of borders and lawns.

The RHS relished this opportunity to pursue the Robinsons' work, showing visitors that with vision and determination you can create a wonderful garden whatever the conditions. Hyde Hall has become a centre of horticultural excellence and experimentation, and is taking the lead as Britain faces the challenge of gardening in a changing climate.

One of the first RHS operations was excavating a 45-million litre/10-million gallon reservoir for irrigation. As befits an ethos of water efficiency, rainwater from the new car park and visitor centre (completed in 2009) drains into the reservoir. Other environmentally friendly initiatives include a ground source heat pump for the visitor centre and recycled concrete aggregate for the approach road.

Existing areas at Hyde Hall proved that you can create a garden by modifying growing conditions with shelter belts and by improving the soil with plenty of organic matter. But what about gardening *with* the conditions? The RHS set itself the challenge and the Dry Garden, showcasing drought-tolerant plants, was completed in 2001 (following, as luck would have it, one of the wettest winters recorded) and then doubled in size in 2011. The policy remains that plants are watered until they become established, then left to rely on natural rainfall.

Created using 260 tonnes of Scottish gabbro boulders to form rocky outcrops, the Dry Garden was laid out over 1,600 square metres/0.4 acres on a south-facing, clay-lined slope. Subsoil was layered on a rubble base. Topsoil was mixed with sand and grit to create a free-draining medium, then mulched with 70 tonnes of rounded flint gravel to conserve moisture and reflect light. The garden today contains more than 400 species from places with low summer rainfall, including the Mediterranean, South Africa, South America and Australia.

A large path weaving through has several narrower paths that branch into the vegetation so visitors can immerse themselves in the landscape and study the plants more closely. There are annuals, grasses, shrubs and succulents. Many are familiar, like euphorbias, artemisias and *Verbena bonariensis*, but others are less so. The choice of plants intentionally pushes the boundaries of accepted hardiness,

although losses in harsh winters has led to some fixed parameters: 70 per cent of plants are reliably hardy, 20 per cent generally considered borderline hardy and 10 per cent are more experimental and tender. Accepting the failures (and the occasional pleasant surprise) is a necessary part of this continuing experiment. By challenging the received wisdom, Hyde Hall is widening the range of plants thought suitable for a dry garden.

In fact, it would seem that Hyde Hall is constantly renewing itself in a way that responds to wider changes. Clover Hill's naturalistic feel reflects current interest in this style of planting. The grasses and herbaceous perennials flowing down the slope are chosen for their tendency to sway in a breeze. Planting at the foot of the hill is in muted pastels, with warmer tones near the top, the whole blending with the seasonal changes in surrounding countryside.

In 2002 the old Pig Park was planted in an informal style with meandering paths and rambling roses. With the blessing of Her Majesty the Queen, this new garden was named in honour of the Queen Mother, a former patron of the RHS.

The Global Growth Vegetable Garden (supported by Witan Investment Trust), at the site's highest point, encourages us to expand the horizons of what we grow and eat. Designed by Xa Tollemache and completed in 2017, it was inspired by the multicultural culinary delights of the 2012 Olympic Games. Surrounding a central glasshouse, the garden's circular layout represents the four quarters of the globe, where crops in curved beds are grouped by geographic origin.

Visitors are introduced to a wealth of edibles that can all be grown fresh at home. There are ancient Andean crops: oca (*Oxalis tuberosa*) and dahlias for their comestible tubers; achocha (*Cyclanthera pedata*),

## Colours and tastes

Walk around RHS gardens like Hyde Hall and you will notice similar colours in different locations. In the glasshouse, you can find tomato 'Gold Nugget' (below left), an early, golden cherry tomato with a well-balanced, delicious flavour. Look outdoors and you will find the crab apple *Malus* 'Butterball' (below right), a pretty, small, spreading tree with slightly drooping branches. In spring the foliage is grey-green, and pink flower buds open to white flowers infused with pink. The fruit is yellow-orange flushed with red. A change of mindset sees both as edible and ornamental. Eat the fruit of the tomato in salads and make the crab apples into jelly.

Opposite, above: Substantial planting alongside the Upper Pond demonstrates how large-leaved plants and vigorous growth can be used successfully to create an impact in unlimited space.

Top: Grass cut at different lengths, as here, on Clover Hill, is a simple way to add definition to the landscape. Long grass around trees also protects them from accidental mower damage.

Above: The Witan Global Growth Vegetable Garden is an opportunity to experiment with lesser-known crops and to reflect the developing needs of twenty-first-century horticulture.

a scrambling climber related to pumpkins that yields small fruits covered in soft spines; and tasty little tomatilloes (*Physalis ixocarpa* and *P. philadelphica*). There are Chinese yams (*Dioscorea polystachya*), chickpeas (*Cicer arietinum*) from the Mediterranean and horseradish trees (*Moringa oleifera*) grown in containers for their leaves, seeds and roots. Japanese, Thai and West Indian cuisines are represented by curly perilla (*Perilla frutescens* var. *crispa*), turmeric (*Curcuma longa*) and callaloo (*Amaranthus* species). In the greenhouse, adzuki beans (*Vigna angularis*), anise (*Pimpinella anisum*), cumin (*Cuminum cyminum*) and kiwano (*Cucumis metuliferus*) tempt the grower.

Each quarter of the vegetable garden is run on a three-year rotation, so it frequently offers new interest to returning visitors. In 2017, for example, a spectacular array of beans for drying revealed the beauty and diversity of North American legumes. A series of more conventional allotment plots is planned for the future, geared towards methods of producing food all year.

Among the newest features at Hyde Hall is the Winter Garden, completed in 2018. Bark texture, stem and twig colour, rustling seed heads and the structural forms of spent herbaceous perennials lift the spirits even in the dreariest of months. The garden includes around 100 types of dogwood with coloured stems (*Cornus* species), part of an RHS trial to establish a new set of recommended AGM selections. Another enhancement is the Welcome Building, which makes the entrance to the garden more spacious and attractive, incorporating a visitor centre, cafe and retail space.

Now that Hyde Hall attracts more than 300,000 visitors annually, the old farm buildings have made way for the Gardeners Rest Restaurant. Its menu incorporates produce from the Global Growth

'Created using 260 tonnes of Scottish gabbro boulders to form rocky outcrops, the Dry Garden was laid out over 1,600 square metres/0.4 acres on a south-facing, clay-lined slope.'

The Dry Garden at Hyde Hall, one of the finest in the country, is filled with plants of all kinds that thrive in the world's Mediterranean climates.

Vegetable Garden, winning the 'Field to Fork' category in the *Essex Life* Food and Drink Awards 2017. The Hilltop Lodge events space, adjoining the restaurant to the south, has magnificent views over the garden and rolling landscape. To the north, the new Clore Learning Centre has a teaching garden with themed sections, such as plants for pollinators and alpines. The centre can accommodate double the previous number of visiting schoolchildren, bringing the figure to around 10,000 per year. By providing space for children to play, fly kites and explore, including the exciting Higgledy Hyde woodland tower, Hyde Hall is hoping to welcome more parents with children.

The Sky Meadow is a long-term commitment to developing perennial and native meadowland. The first sowing, across 7 hectares/17 acres, took place in 2015. Radiating out from an ancient oak on the east of the hill, it will be planted with African, North American and European species that peak from early to late summer, including agapanthus, echinaceas, panicums, euphorbias and kniphofias. Using techniques for establishing different types of meadow, it will offer visitors a glimpse of meadow diversity and eventually connect with the woodland fringes on the outskirts of the estate. The low-rise planting with grass pathways winding through it will allow visitors to enjoy the vast Essex skyscapes and glorious distant views.

Hyde Hall is surrounded by a sea of arable farmland but the periphery of the estate is a wildwood refuge for wildlife. Planting began in 1998 after a fundraising appeal, and continues annually. Over 60,000 trees, hedgerows restored to the positions they once occupied, and a meadow flowing down to the reservoir and woodland beyond, have created different habitats and dramatically influenced the local

flora and fauna. Southern marsh, pyramidal, common spotted and green-winged orchids flourish. In 2017 a spurge hawkmoth caterpillar was believed to be the first recorded in Essex since 1872.

On becoming responsible for the Robinsons' garden, the RHS drew up a Hyde Hall masterplan incorporating a vision for its future. Pre-existing elements, like the hilltop beds and herbaceous borders, have either been expanded, replanted, revived or altered. The garden is constantly on the move. The Australia and New Zealand Garden adjoins the Queen Mother's Garden. A Millennium Avenue of eighty *Quercus frainetto* interspersed with *Fraxinus excelsior* 'Westhof's Glorie' now links the west and east of the site. In 2010, a new lake was excavated and the surroundings planted with trees for spring and autumn colour. Two connected courtyard gardens – a traditional cottage garden and a modern country garden – were created as a setting for the Welcome Building.

As the largest RHS garden, with 148 hectares/365 acres providing plenty of space, Hyde Hall will continue to improve and evolve at a pace. There are plans to plant hundreds more trees to form an arboretum, and a Mediterranean garden marked by massed swathes of plantings across the undulating landscape will complement the special nature of this extraordinary site. Through all the changes, the garden continues to bear tribute to the remarkable Robinsons, in particular their love of plants as well as gritty determination.

RHS Chelsea Flower Show is full
of innovation, excitement and
happy gardeners.

Chapter 8
# The shows must go on ...

# The shows must go on ...

Thousands of gardeners look forward to RHS shows every year. The British love a show and love gardening, and how could they resist? Over time, the shows have expanded from focusing entirely on plants, gardens and horticultural accessories into events where you can bring your children and non-gardening friends for a great day out. There is inspiration for anyone who loves cookery, classic cars, or even stylish shopping in the *Country Living* marquees.

The tradition that began with the society's earliest shows in Kensington and Chiswick has blossomed into twelve shows in fabulous locations around Britain, each with their own character, including the latest addition at the Chatsworth estate in Derbyshire. Shows are a way for the RHS to engage with their members and the general public, delighting visitors with an exceptional experience and inspiring everyone to get out and garden through displays of world-leading horticulture.

Chelsea, the greatest of all, held every May in the grounds of the Royal Hospital in central London, has grown beyond a flower show for plant and garden lovers to become a firmly established must-visit event, alongside Royal Ascot or Wimbledon. The Gold medals and Best in Show awards carry considerable cachet. Chelsea still creates a sense of excitement unlike any other, and that same focus on style and quality is now maintained in all the shows hosted by the RHS.

The season kicks off in April with Cardiff. The show at Tatton Park has a distinctive glamour of its own, and the Malvern shows are renowned for innovation and the autumnal display of giant vegetables. There is a unique sense of history at Hampton Court, where the backdrop of the palace creates a truly magisterial aura for the show held here in July, and large crowds seem to fade magically into the foliage.

While times are changing for the London shows, which have such stories to tell, the RHS gardens each now have their own event and these are proving increasingly popular.

Visitors flock to shows largely to be inspired by the show gardens in their many guises, as well as for the chance to buy rare and distinctive plants. The floral marquees are always filled with a dazzling array of specialist nurseries, whose owners are passionate plantspeople, willing to dispense hard-earned cultural advice to ensure their precious plants thrive in your garden. It is hard not to give way to temptation.

One of the most fascinating moments must be the sell-off on the final day, when people scrabble to bag a bargain, sometimes with little thought as to how they will take it home. It is not unusual to see giant bamboos sprout legs and head off towards the Tube station at Chelsea or convertible cars become transformed into mobile herbaceous borders. The RHS shows, in all their glory, encapsulate much that is quaint and quirky about Britain. They are such a delicious mixture of plants, eccentricity and fun.

Left: The glazed roofs of the RHS Horticultural Halls in Westminster enable gardeners to evaluate plants in natural light before deciding which to buy.

Right: Among the attractions at the RHS London Harvest Festival in 2017 was a beautiful display showing a tempting range of chillies.

# RHS London shows

The vast cathedral-like spaces of the RHS Lawrence and Lindley Halls in Westminster are horticulture's holy places, where past and present entwine. The halls provide a powerful link with the old days when legendary nurseries would create displays of flamboyant showmanship, tempting aristocrats to buy plants for their gardens from the paradise conjured up by the London shows. Until the early 1990s, the large rhododendron nurseries still staged breathtakingly beautiful and large-scale displays at the spring shows. There is a real sense of history and knowledge here.

Traditionally, the great shows were in the spring and autumn, when the plants favoured by the aristocracy reached their peak. Head gardeners arrived in spring with alpines, magnolias, rhododendrons and camellias. They returned for the Great Autumn Show with displays of leaves, berries and fruit, gathered from the arboreta of the likes of Lord Aberconway from Bodnant Gardens; the Rothschilds at Exbury; the Williamses of Caerhays; and from John Bond, Keeper of The Crown Estate, Windsor.

From the time the Lindley Hall opened in 1904 until the 1980s, the London shows were held fortnightly with a gap at Christmas and around the dates of the summer flower shows. After that time, there were various combinations, with around eight shows a year plus the RHS National Orchid Show in March and the RHS Great Autumn Show in October. There were also additional shows like the Landscape Show and the Christmas Shows from 1993 to 2001 – when exhibitors were seen in fancy dress and reindeer made an appearance – and the Urban Garden Show from 2016 to 2018. The regular shows took on various themes. For example, in 2006 there were Houseplants (January), Fashion in the Garden (February), Unusual Spring Bulbs (March),

Tulips around the World (April) and Winter Greenery (November). Three London shows that year also featured botanical art. By 2012 this was concentrated in one show, usually in spring.

RHS committee members of a certain vintage go misty eyed at the recollection of past glories, particularly the early spring show, when the scent of bulbs regaled the senses as you set foot in the foyer of New Hall (as Lawrence Hall, completed in 1928, used to be called). It was similar in autumn, when the Lindley Hall was transformed into an oversized village show with hundreds of plates of colourful fruit, grown to perfection, and a ripe fragrance filled the hall.

Produce has always been a major feature in early October, at what has become known as the RHS London Harvest Show. In 2004, the bicentenary of the RHS was celebrated with a display of 200 different apples and pears. Another memorable occasion was the centenary of the 1883 National Apple Congress in 1983, which was observed with an exhibition of regional apples and a selection of pears from RHS Garden Wisley and the National Fruit Collection at Brogdale, Kent.

In October 2015, Adrian Baggaley exceeded his previous achievements by winning thirty-five of the forty classes he entered in the Autumn Fruit and Vegetable Competition, including the Best Dish of Apples, the Best Dish of Pears and, most challenging of all, Best Collection of Fruit, a total of nine perfectly matched, flawless dishes of apples and pears.

One of the classes is glasshouse grapes. In the past, there were entries from all of the great estates, although now there are only three or four, notably from the dukes of Devonshire and Marlborough, who have competed with one another for decades with 'Muscat of Alexandria', 'Mrs Pince's Black Muscat' and 'Muscat Hamburg'.

Perfect plates of potatoes, carrots and onions have always been open for admiration at the vegetable competition. In recent years, Mrs Sherrie Plumb has won the RHS Vegetable Cup three times and the Ridell Trophy for Vegetables five times. The record for the Giant Pumpkin Competition at the Harvest Show is Ian Paton's 2013 entry weighing in at 620 kilograms/1,367 pounds.

Ornamental plants are the mainstay of the shows. When Irish daffodil breeders first attended the London shows in 1914, they brought their plants packed in wooden boxes on the ferry, travelled down to London on the overnight sleeper and went straight to the halls to start staging. It became known to them as the Guy Wilson Trail, after the breeder who first made the journey.

In February 2000, John Massey of Ashwood Nurseries collaborated

> 'The halls provide a powerful link with the old days when legendary nurseries would create displays of flamboyant showmanship, tempting aristocrats to buy plants for their gardens from the paradise conjured up by the London shows.'

with Niigata Nursery Association of Japan to create a gorgeous display of *Hepatica* on waist-height staging. The circular display was divided in half: on one side the plants were displayed as they would be in nature, and, on the other, in traditional Japanese style in pots – something never seen before in the West. Visitors arrived from far afield, including the United States and Sweden, and the queue was hundreds of yards long. The hall was so full that entry had to be restricted. The display won Gold and the Lawrence Medal for the best exhibit of the year. A great impression was also made in 1992 by John Bond's display of mahonias from the National Collection, placed in vases all along one wall. It delighted the connoisseurs and won the Williams Memorial Medal.

The vibrantly coloured displays of dahlia specialists Roger and Hazel Aylett were unforgettable for their 'flower power'. After winning their first Gold medal in 1961, they went on to win a further fifty-four in consecutive years and the Williams Memorial Medal three times. Attending the fortnightly shows in London from the beginning of the dahlia flowering season until the Great Autumn Show, they were regularly allocated what fellow exhibitors considered to be the premier site in the New Hall – the stand under the clock, facing everyone who entered. There could be between fifty and eighty vases, each containing forty blooms of one variety at the same stage of maturity. They were arranged so every bloom could be viewed individually or collectively as a complete display. In the early days of exhibiting there were over thirty different dahlia exhibitors, but by 1999 there were only one or two left.

Sometimes successes were achieved using unorthodox materials. Roy Lancaster and Tom Beynes from Hillier Nurseries created in 1966 a Gold medal-winning exhibit of fungi, displayed as they would be found in nature, on rotting logs with accompanying shrubs. Among

Far left: Said to be the tallest in England at the time, a specimen of *Rhododendron falconeri*, over 6 metres/20 feet tall, was displayed at the Rhododendron Association Show on 2–3 May 1933 by Messrs Gill Nursery. The man in the hat is Mr Richard Gill. Don't let go of the ladder.

Left: Dahlias go in and out of fashion but have a core of devoted admirers.

Above: One of the greatest challenges is lifting and weighing giant pumpkins. The secret is not to drop it.

Right: It raises the spirits to see so much perfectly grown fruit in one place; both the quality and aroma are memorable.

Right, below: You may know your onions, but what about your potatoes? Displays like this allow gardeners to compare, contrast and be amazed.

Left, top: Nurseries have to be both accomplished growers and good at staging plants. Those with an artistic eye know exactly how to show off all their virtues.

Left, bottom: The RHS shows are opportunities for nurseries to introduce new plants. Gardeners are likely to be familiar with pleiones, but less so with hardy hybrid cymbidiums.

Top: Visitors marvelling at the skill of the botanical artists at the RHS London Orchid and Botanical Art Show 2012.

Above: Lost in London? The awning above a door tells you exactly where you are.

the collection were fly agaric, stinkhorn, honey fungus and the death cap, which had been collected around the New Forest and kept for the weekend before the show in an Anderson shelter. On the way to Westminster they stopped at the Royal Botanic Gardens, Kew, where a mycologist identified several species unknown to them.

For many years, the British Orchid Growers' Association Show was held annually, in mid-March. In the early days, the great Victorian orchid nurseries, including Sanders of St Albans, McBean's Orchids, Veitch's Royal Exotic Nursery and aristocrats like Baron Schroeder and the Duke of Devonshire all exhibited regularly. In 2000, the Orchid Show boasted twelve UK amateur orchid societies and fifty-five exhibitors from around the world, including representatives from several countries in continental Europe, North and South America, and China. Over 6,000 people came to the show, including visitors from Holland, Germany, France and Spain. In 2002, Japanese orchid grower and potter Shunji Mitsuhashi displayed Japanese native orchids next to copies of paintings published 160 years ago. Some of the original plants shown in the paintings were still growing in his collection.

From 2019 there will be fewer Westminster shows each year, the remainder moving to RHS gardens, where they attract larger audiences. Although the London shows currently receive a total of 12,000 visitors a year, they rely on the RHS's charitable funds to run, and exhibitors have to contend with the high costs of the congestion charge and parking, as well as increasing hotel prices. Although practical and economic factors – including the rental income of the Lawrence Hall to finance new projects – have caused the shows to migrate to the regional gardens, the RHS London Flower Shows will always be the heart and soul of the past.

# RHS Chelsea Flower Show

The first Great Spring Show took place in 1862 at the RHS garden in Kensington – on the site of what is now the Science Museum. When this garden closed in 1888, the show moved to the gardens of the Inner Temple, where it remained until 1911. The RHS cancelled the show in 1912 so that it could work with other organisations to stage the Royal Horticultural Exhibition in the grounds of the Royal Hospital, Chelsea. This proved to be such an excellent site that the Great Spring Show moved there the following year, and what we know now as the RHS Chelsea Flower Show was born. Originally attended by landowners, their wives and head gardeners, these days it is thronged with members of the public from all backgrounds. It is without a doubt a highlight of the global gardening calendar.

The show has been held every year, except for 1917 and 1918 and the duration of the Second World War, when the War Office commandeered the land for an anti-aircraft battery. Initially, the show ran for three days, but in 1925 it became five days, before reverting back to three again after exhibitors complained that five days was too long. A fourth day was added in 1933 and a fifth in 2005.

From the outset, it was a very popular and well-attended show, and as early as the 1950s there were complaints about overcrowding. In 1987, after the turnstiles had to be closed because of the crowds, the RHS Council took the momentous decision that entry could no longer be by RHS membership card, but by ticket only. Visitors were limited to 40,000 a day.

In the early days, exhibitors were mainly from nurseries and country house gardens, whose owners and head gardeners put on displays to demonstrate their horticultural prowess. However, during the twentieth century, country house horticulture became less significant and the last exhibitor of this kind was Maurice Mason, of Talbot Manor, Norfolk. He won the Lawrence Medal for the best exhibit in 1980, for a display of exotic plants from his glasshouses. Today, the show is divided into three main categories: nurseries, show gardens and sundries (these are the trade stands, selling goods as diverse as greenhouses, gardening gloves and statues).

The first show gardens appeared in the spring shows of the 1890s, when nurseries specialising in alpines were permitted to construct small rock gardens in the open air to display their plants. Japanese gardens and gardens incorporating trees and shrubs soon followed, and by the era of the first Chelsea show the format was well established. During the first half of the twentieth century, rock gardens were the dominant theme with everything else in the catalogue labelled as a 'formal garden'. Most of the gardens were created by nurseries, although some professional garden designers promoted their skills. In 1961, the magazine *Popular Gardening* created 'The Garden of Today' – the first show garden to be sponsored by an outside organisation.

In its early incarnation, the Chelsea show was held in a series of tents, but in 1951 these were replaced with a single great marquee – listed in the *Guinness Book of Records* as the world's largest tent. In 2000, this was replaced by the Great Pavilion, which is so large that 500 London buses could be parked inside.

The Great Pavilion is the domain of smaller specialist nurseries, displaying anything from alpines to trees, bamboos and bougainvilleas. It is here that Beth Chatto won ten consecutive Gold medals; Beatrix Havergal created her legendary displays of strawberry 'Sovereign'; and Harry Wheatcroft and David Austin exhibited their world-famous roses. Raymond Evison has garnered many Golds fo his exhibits of clematis,

Johnny Walkers continues to amaze with his displays of *Narcissus*, and Matt Soper, Jekka McVicar and Medwyn Williams have each regularly staged outstanding exhibits of carnivorous plants, herbs and vegetables. Hillier Nurseries traditionally exhibit in the centre of the Great Pavilion, around the Chilianwalla Monument, where they have won most of their seventy-two consecutive Gold medals – and a place in the record books.

There are also exhibits by local authorities. In 1996, Birmingham City Council exhibited a motor car made out of plants to celebrate 100 years of British motoring, and they returned in 2018 with a display to celebrate the legacy of the Windrush generation. Only three nurseries still remain who took part in the original Chelsea show: Kelways, renowned for their peonies; Blackmore & Langdon, famed for their fabulous displays of delphiniums and begonias; and McBean's Orchids.

Over the years, there have been exhibitors from every continent, such as the Horticultural Society of Trinidad and Tobago, the Barbados Horticultural Society and the Kirstenbosch Botanical Garden, South Africa. In May 1960, the Malayan Orchid Society displayed more than 1,600 sprays of cut orchids flown from Singapore. Cut orchids were relatively new at the time and made quite an impact, as well as earning a Gold medal. The vibrant and flamboyant displays of Thailand's Nongnooch Tropical Botanical Garden have based their decorations on the architecture of Buddhist temples since 2012.

Right from the beginning, the show has included garden tools and equipment, and these have also changed with the times. The first aluminium glasshouses appeared in the 1950s and the first drip irrigation systems in the 1980s. Over time, garden ladders have evolved from wood to aluminium, and glasshouse heaters from old cast-iron boilers to gas and electric-fan heaters.

Some of the most memorable show gardens on the main avenue have been created by popular garden designer Diarmuid Gavin. In 2011 he presented his Gold medal-winning 'Irish Sky Garden', built in a pink ovoid container and suspended 25 metres/82 feet above the ground; and in 2012 he designed 'The Westland Magical Tower Garden', a seven-storey stepped pyramid, 24 metres/79 feet tall, made from black scaffolding with gold fixings, and featuring a lift and a slide. This was followed in 2016 by his 'British Eccentrics Garden', inspired by the work of cartoonist William Heath Robinson, with automated, bopping box hedges, twirling conical bays and spinning circular beds.

Chelsea has long been a showcase for the greats of garden design, including John Brookes, Sylvia Crowe and Russell Page. More recently, there have been many creative contributions from Chris Beardshaw, Christopher Bradley-Hole, Sarah Eberle, Luciano Giubbilei, Arne Maynard, Gavin McWilliam, Piet Oudolf, Dan Pearson, Roger Platts, Sarah Price, David Stevens, Andy Sturgeon, Tom Stuart-Smith, Jo Thompson, Cleve West and Andrew Wilson. Newer talents to watch for in future shows include Tom Massey, David and Harry Rich and Will Williams.

Controversy is never far away. Paul Cooper's 'Constructivist Garden' in 1994 was not awarded a medal, for it was deemed too radical; James May's 'Paradise in Plasticine' garden in 2009 won a plasticine medal and divided opinion; and Sarah Eberle's 2007 'Life on Mars' was simply a garden for an astronaut. The appearance of artificial grass in Tony Smith's 'Urban Plantaholic's Kitchen Garden' in 2010 was a shock for traditionalists, but perhaps a sign of things to come. Phillip Johnson's staggering 2016 installation was a hand-crocheted red carpet of almost 300,000 poppies between the showground and the Royal Hospital.

Left: Visitors outside the marquee at the Chelsea Flower Show in 1953; it was still a grand, formal affair.

Left, below: Some of the most memorable exhibits in recent years have been by the Nongnooch Tropical Botanical Garden from Thailand, with their extravagant displays of orchids.

Right, top: Photographers are among the first to arrive in the early mornings, as this image from 2012 proves.

Right, bottom: In 2017, Hillier Nurseries' 'Spring' garden, designed by Sarah Eberle, explored every definition of the word. The display included seasonal flowers and a large metal coil.

Left: The attention to detail and creative skill demonstrated in the Artisan Gardens category was exemplified in 'A Hebridean Weaver's Garden' in 2013.

Left, below: Designers sometimes tackle challenging subjects: 'The Imperial Garden – Revive' in the Fresh category, 2016, explored the complex relationship between Russia, Ukraine and the United Kingdom.

Above: In 2017, the 'Commonwealth War Graves Commission Centenary Garden' featured a convex mirror in the hedge, so that visitors could see their reflections and take time to reflect.

Right: The Chelsea Flower Show gives both garden designers and metalworkers an opportunity to express themselves.

'Trendspotters are eager to get a first glimpse of Chelsea on Press Day, to see what themes the show gardens are going with that may influence the season ahead.'

The smaller Artisan Gardens first appeared in 2011, with the aim of encouraging a variety of designs for the small garden, while also being packed full of planting ideas, quirky features, fastidious attention to detail and exquisite craftsmanship. There were also the Fresh Gardens, whose aim was to give garden designers an opportunity to use their creativity to redefine perceptions and expectations of a garden space. Embracing new technology and cutting-edge design, they are made to provoke thought and encourage debate. James Basson's 2013 garden 'After the Fire', for example, showed native plants regenerating among blackened soil following a wildfire. Its realism was electrifying, and it won Best in Show in the Fresh category for that year.

As part of the Chelsea centenary celebrations in 2013, French iris grower Cayeux demonstrated how irises dating from 1913 compared with modern varieties, and the Chelsea Plant of the Year competition, which began in 2010, was renamed Plant of the Century. Ten plants were selected – one from each decade – and then put to a public vote online. The winner was *Geranium* Rozanne ('Gerwat').

The centenary also produced a plethora of products: a Union Jack of flowers, fridge magnets, tea towels, limited-edition handmade mugs and garden benches, and a T-shirt celebrating 100 years of Chelsea. On the showground, Best in Show was awarded to 'The Australian Garden' designed by Phillip Johnson – the first garden from that continent ever to win this honour. As the designer was an advocate of sustainable gardening, he used only rainwater in the pool and waterfall, which he collected from the roof of the BBC tent.

The press tent is always a hive of activity on Press Day, held on the Monday before the show opens. It allows the world's media to experience the show for themselves and spot celebrities and stars of television, film and the music world. Her Majesty the Queen and other members of the royal family visit annually, amid tight security, at the close of the Press Day and before the Gala Preview evening.

Trendspotters are eager to get a first glimpse of Chelsea on Press Day, to see what themes the show gardens are going with that may influence the season ahead. In past years it has been rhododendrons in the 'Surrey' style, cottage gardens, decking and painted walls. Copper-flowered *Verbascum* 'Helen Johnson', which was found as a chance seedling on the rock gardens at the Royal Botanic Gardens, Kew, became the 'must-have' plant in the 1990s, and lupins were the perennial cottage garden favourite in 2018.

Whatever the themes, RHS rules have always stated that 'highly coloured figures including animals, birds, gnomes, fairies or any

Left, top: Visitors flock to the show gardens along Main Avenue. The 2017 'Morgan Stanley Garden' was inspired by the fractal geometry and patterns found in nature, music, art and social communities.

Left, bottom: The 2016 Gold medal-winning 'Senri-Sentei – Garage Garden', designed by Kazuyuki Ishihara for a classic car enthusiast, put the garden on a garage roof.

Above: Garden designer Chris Beardshaw is a multi-Gold medallist at Chelsea. Several of his gardens have been rebuilt at new locations after the show.

Above right, top: Shows information staff are always ready to help visitors, and it sometimes needs a team effort.

Above right, bottom: Queen Elizabeth views a floral tribute to her, designed by florist Veevers Carter, during her visit to Chelsea in 2016.

similar creatures actual or mythical, for use as garden ornaments' are not to appear at any show. In 2013, however, gnomes were allowed at Chelsea for the first time. These were decorated by Dame Maggie Smith, Sir Elton John, Dame Helen Mirren and other well-known personalities, and were sold on eBay to raise funds for the RHS Chelsea Centenary Appeal in support of school gardening.

In 2018, the RHS 'Feel Good Garden' was designed by Matt Keightley and highlighted the importance of gardening for health and wellbeing, mirroring the gardens he is creating at Wisley on the same theme. The garden was organic in shape, so visitors felt relaxed, and the seating areas were designed to be discovered as you meandered around the garden at your own pace, enjoying the soft colours. After the show it was rebuilt at the Highgate Mental Health Centre, and the RHS has pledged two more Chelsea gardens in 2019 and 2020 for use by NHS patients. There was also a Gardening for Health Forum at the show, where health professionals and members of the RHS explored ways to promote non-medical solutions – or social prescribing – alongside traditional treatments.

Chelsea continues to be an exciting mix of cutting-edge and tradition, a place to see and be seen, overflowing with inspiration from the best horticulture has to offer. Here, the spotlight shines for one week of the year on the greatest and most prestigious flower show in the world.

In 2017 Manoj Malde's 'Inland Homes: Beneath a Mexican Sky', with vivid colour-washed walls and drought-tolerant plants, was inspired by the famous Mexican architect Luis Barragán.

# RHS Malvern Spring Festival and Autumn Show

The flower show at Hampton Court has its palace, and Chatsworth its stately home, but nothing can quite compare with the picturesque setting of the RHS shows at Malvern against the glorious backdrop of the Malvern Hills. A spectacular, ever-changing scene according to the light and season, it is a tapestry of fresh green in spring followed by glowing golds and yellows in the early autumn sun. This has to be the perfect place for a flower show.

The two Malvern shows, in spring and autumn, are held at the Three Counties Showground, an immaculately maintained expanse of bright green grass surrounded by post-and rail-fencing. When filled with marquees, show gardens and an added dash of 'lifestyle', it has the lively atmosphere of an up-market county show.

For many years known as the Malvern Spring Gardening Show, this collaboration between the Three Counties Agricultural Society and the RHS first became known as the RHS Malvern Spring Festival in 2014. This brought the RHS to the fore and drew the focus firmly on to gardening and food, in an attempt to boost declining visitor numbers. It worked. Attendance at the spring show in 2014 of 90,000 had risen to an all-time high of over 100,000 by 2018.

The spring show, an early-season opportunity to buy plants, is filled with visitors in search of horticultural retail therapy. Their wish is granted by numerous stands in the Plant Village and the UK's longest floral marquee, which at over 190 metres/625 feet long – the equivalent of four Olympic swimming pools – houses up to one hundred nurseries. A joy to behold when awash with early-season colour, it is heady with the fragrance of plants and alive with animated conversation between passionate plantspeople and stallholders. There is a strong regional feel, with many local exhibitors and nurseries such as Fuchsiavale

from Kidderminster, Chris Cooke Plants from Cheltenham, and Fibrex Nurseries from Stratford-upon-Avon.

The Spring Festival is also renowned for its gardens. The Green Living Spaces category attracts new designers, who can receive a bursary from the RHS and help from mentors including celebrated designers Paul Hervey-Brookes, Jo Thompson and RHS Ambassador Jamie Butterworth. They can express their creativity in any way they choose, using any type of plants and materials, before the designs go through the RHS selection process; the best are then chosen for the show. They provide inspiration for balcony, courtyard and patio gardens, offering take-home ideas for people with limited space.

A source of inspiration for young gardeners is the School Garden Challenge, whose past mentors include designer Chris Beardshaw and former BBC *Blue Peter* gardener Chris Collins. After the theme for each year is announced, they run workshops to help children create a design linked to the national curriculum, and to grow the plants for their gardens. Young gardeners, from home-schooled children to teenagers at college, then build their gardens at the showground. In 2018, the theme 'Celebrating Everything that's Great about Britain' showcased a range of subjects, including the work of Isambard Kingdom Brunel and a garden based on the British Sunday lunch.

Several well-known designers took their early steps at Malvern, among them Diarmuid Gavin and Paul Hervey-Brookes, who presented their first show gardens in 2001 and 2008 respectively. Visitors can expect to see between five and ten show gardens at each of the shows, and these include gardens by a group of stalwarts known to show staff as 'the big three': Jason Hales, Peter Dowle and the Graduate Gardeners – who have all scooped a succession of Gold medals and Best in Shows.

Jason Hales of Villaggio Verde creates remarkable cameos of the Mediterranean. More stage-set than garden, his 2013 design 'Reposer Vos Roues' (Rest Your Wheels), depicted a rustic cafe – a refreshment stop on the route of the Tour de France, which had hosted professional cyclists for more than 100 years. The 2014 garden 'En su Casa en la Playa' (At Home on the Beach) was possibly the largest RHS show garden ever built, and it instantly transported visitors to a beachside retreat in the Balearic Islands, complete with a garden, boat and paella hut. In 2018, 'Billy's Cave' envisaged part of a smallholding in rural Portugal, with a cave, natural spring and goat paddock. It was bordered by old olive trees and the herder's wife's garden, full of shrubs, aromatic herbs and fruit trees. Two pygmy goats and their kids – including one called Billy – became unexpected stars of the show.

Nurseryman and garden designer Peter Dowle's mastery is in using the borrowed landscape of the Malvern Hills. This was typified in his garden 'A Japanese Reflection' in 2016, which was an exquisitely executed collaboration with Richard Jasper. His 2018 'Spirit of the Woods' garden featured the work of sculptor Simon Gudgeon, a stone grotto and a ballerina made from more than 1,000 copper leaves.

The Graduate Gardeners won their fifth Gold medal and Best in Show for the third year running in 2014 for their design 'Bringing Nature Home'. This was a contemporary formal garden leading out to a wildflower meadow. The garden was split into areas by a framework of corten-steel beams filled with battens made from western red cedar. Raindrops fell from a steel beam into a reflective pool, creating ripples on the water's surface.

For visitors interested in growing their own, inspiration can always be found among the show bench displays of perfect vegetables by Medwyn Williams as well as the model allotments and kitchen gardens of award-winning edible garden designer Jon Wheatley. There are also talks on practical vegetable growing from the likes of Christine Walkden from The One Show and gardening personality Jim Buttress, and in the Cookery Theatre, gardener-cook Mark Diacono from Otter Farm is a regular host, as well as RHS Ambassador Mary Berry and other celebrity chefs.

The festival green draws crowds at the spring show with displays of classic cars and an arts market. At the autumn show, there are children's competitions, such as designing a garden on a plate or arts and crafts using fruit, vegetables and pasta. The biggest attraction of

'The flower show at Hampton Court has its palace, and Chatsworth its stately home, but nothing can quite compare with the picturesque setting of the RHS shows at Malvern.'

Left, top: 'The Spirit of the Woods', designed by Peter Dowle for the RHS Malvern Spring Festival in 2018, borrowed the landscape of the Malvern Hills beyond.

Left, bottom: The floral marquee is full of plants and take-home ideas, such as troughs and pots for displaying alpine plants.

Below: In 2015, 'An Andalusian Moment' by Villaggio Verde won Gold and Best Show Garden at the Malvern Spring Festival.

Right: 'Bringing Nature Home', a show garden at Malvern Spring Festival in 2014, featured an attractive sitting area and comfortable chairs.

Left: Hannah Genders designed 'The Journey Garden' for St Michael's Hospice at the Spring Festival in 2015, reflecting the many challenges faced during illness and loss.

Bottom: 'At One With... A Meditation Garden', designed by Peter Dowle and Richard Jasper, was a quiet retreat designed for meditation, yoga or simply a place to relax. There is an aura of calm, despite the crowds.

Below: 'A Woodland Kitchen Garden', including vegetable beds of sorrel, beetroot and ruby chard, was both edible and ornamental.

Right: The Green Living Spaces category demonstrates that it is possible to have a beautiful garden, even in the smallest of spaces. This area was designed by RHS Ambassador Jamie Butterworth.

all, however, is the popular National Giant Vegetables Championship, which has seen a marked increase in entries over the last five years, attracting almost 600 entries in 2018.

The vegetable entries are so large, it is no surprise to see them arriving in vans, forklifts and flatbed trucks. They are certainly too big for a barrow. In 2015, Joe Atherton from Mansfield grew the world's longest beetroot, which measured 7.956 metres/26.102 feet (and was 75 centimetres/30 inches longer than the previous record), the world's longest parsnip measuring 5.023 metres/16.479 feet, and the world's longest carrot at 6.245 metres/2.489 feet. What a tremendous return for a single year.

In 2016, the world's heaviest red cabbage was presented by grower David Thomas from Hayle in Cornwall; it weighed in at 23.3 kilograms/51.4 pounds, almost 5 kilograms/11 pounds heavier than the previous record set in 1925. He gave some seed to his friend, Tim Saint, who then beat him by 0.4 kilograms/0.9 pounds in 2018 with a monster red cabbage weighing 23.7 kilograms/52.2 pounds – the same as an average seven-year-old child.

There were four new world records in 2017, a new European record and two British records. In 2018, there were six new world records, the first of which – the world's heaviest celery – was broken at midday on the Friday by Sam Purvis from The Old Rectory in Henley, who held the title for five minutes before it was snatched by his boss, Gary Heeks with a super-sized celery weighing in at 42 kilograms/93 pounds, the same as a chimpanzee. Such is the skill of the growers that new challenges were needed, so four new classes have been added, which include the three heaviest sticks of rhubarb, the heaviest aubergine and the longest radish. The sight of these awe-inspiring giants

certainly captures the imagination of visitors, who are fascinated by the sheer size of the vegetables. Some take away ideas and tips from the growers and are inspired to enter their own produce in competitions.

It could be said that both of the RHS shows at Malvern have two faces: stylish and traditional on the surface, but quirky and fun at heart. Jonathan Moseley's romantic 'Floral Fountain' of 2017 and Clare Young's 'Work of Heart' in 2018, which was the world's first knitted garden, are two examples of the different takes on offer. Russian designer Jonas Egger, inspired by Fabergé, created in 2018 the world's first garden inside an egg. This 3.5-metre/11.5-foot tall metal structure opened to music, light, fog and water effects, and then closed. At Malvern, you must expect the unexpected.

Left: Adding a zing to your garden polarises opinions. Whether you love or loathe it depends on your taste.

Right: The scarecrow competitions are always themed; in 2010 it was Shakespeare's comedies.

# RHS Hampton Court Palace Garden Festival

The RHS flower shows are continually developing and being refreshed, ensuring that there is always plenty to see. And occasionally a show is even reborn. In 2019 the RHS's largest show became the RHS Hampton Court Palace Garden Festival, its new name reflecting the host of additional features on offer. Looking back to its creation, this show has in fact evolved through several changes to arrive at its current identity.

The original Hampton Court Palace Flower Show was the brainchild of management consultant Adrian Boyd, in response to cuts in funding to the Historic Royal Palaces. He approached the rail company Network Southeast with the idea that they sponsor a flower show at Hampton Court Palace, for which they could provide the public transport. At the first show in July 1990, railway staff wore carnations in their caps and the stations along the line from Waterloo to Hampton Court were decorated with flowers to send visitors on their way to the show in style. Many visitors still travel by train, others by boat and, on one notable occasion, a lady arrived on a horse. However, in 1992, Network Southeast withdrew its support and a sealed bid from the RHS was accepted in its place.

With the Chelsea Flower Show becoming increasingly popular, the RHS had been searching for a new London site for several years. The location and timing were perfect. Chelsea, a spring show, was small, upmarket, and traditional; Hampton Court was spacious, open to all and took place at the peak of the gardening season. Visitors loved the wide-open spaces, and the walk across the pontoon bridge over the Long Water was a highlight. Perhaps one of the greatest attractions of all was that, for the first time, they could buy plants and accessories at an RHS outdoor show. It remains a great place to shop.

The RHS Hampton Court Palace Flower Show, covering 13 hectares/33 acres, is now the largest annual flower show in the world. While always reflecting current gardening trends, it can be political, controversial and philosophical. At its heart, though, it is all about fun for the family.

The first RHS show at Hampton Court Palace, in 1993, was a resounding success, and some show regulars were soon established. The *Daily Mail*, which co-sponsored shows with the RHS until 2009, created several popular displays in one of the pavilions, which always featured a thatched cottage and garden. The British Rose Festival, which became a major exhibitor in 1991, has adopted some successful themes over the years, including Circus and Romanesque. In their rose-filled marquee, new varieties are launched and advice is available from the experts. The cultivated plant conservation charity, Plant Heritage, first attended in 1992, when thirty-one collection holders displayed plants. They have since introduced a new Malmaison carnation 'James Muir' (2013), highlighted plants on their 'Missing Genera' list (2016), and gathered fourteen Gold medals. At their 40th anniversary in 2018, their president, Alan Titchmarsh, praised the hundreds of plant enthusiasts who dedicate themselves to curating National Plant Collections.

With plenty of room to expand, the RHS Hampton Court Palace Flower Show soon gained a reputation as a place for experimentation and innovation for the sheer variety of gardens on display. Conceptual gardens first appeared in 2006 at one of the hottest, driest shows ever, and these have been a big attraction.

Multiple Gold medal-winner Tony Smith has amazed and bemused visitors in equal measure over the years, particularly in 2008. His garden, 'Ecstasy in a Very Black Box', sought to represent bipolar disorder, using bright green lettuces, shards of coloured perspex and unrolled tarmac, viewed through slits in a matt-black wall. One year, the theme was 'The Seven Deadly Sins'. In response, Rachel Parker

Soden's 'Lust' garden portrayed plants in a 'live show' from the red-light district of Amsterdam, and Sheena Seeks' 'Quarry of Silence' used spades to represent people marching up a mound in search of the great prize, a golden nugget – it won Gold and Best Conceptual Garden. In Nilufer Danis's 'Wrath – Eruption of Unhealed Anger', plants grew in a smoking volcano, which proved to be a huge crowd-pleaser.

The show also creates opportunities for new designers. Cleve West presented his first RHS show garden here in 1994, in an early collaboration with sculptor Johnny Woodford. His self-financed garden 'Homage to the Green Man' was achieved with a small bequest from an aunt, and many of the plants were dug up and transported from his own garden. It was the first ever organic show garden, and it won a Silver-Gilt medal and the George Cooke Memorial Award for the most innovative and imaginative garden.

To launch the new Lifestyle Gardens category in 2018, intended to reflect an owner's personality and way of life, four up-and-coming female designers were invited to take part. This move to encourage new talent also marked 100 years since women were given the right to vote. Reflecting a topical theme, Alexandra Noble created a 'Health and Wellbeing' garden, featuring looping paths and hazy planting for tuning into a state of mindfulness.

Despite the presence of cutting-edge ideas, a traditional spirit remains at this show. Jon Wheatley has created several large-scale displays celebrating traditional British horticulture, notably 'Growing Tastes' with Mary Payne and Terry Porter. This was the first time an allotment won Best in Show at the RHS. More recently, his 2014 'Fifty Golden Years' celebrated Britain in Bloom and was created with the help of volunteers.

Growing your own has been a long-running theme. The 2009 show featured edible front gardens, and in 2012 there were 'Low-Cost, High-Impact' gardens built on budgets ranging from £5,000 to £15,000. Packed with practical ideas, they showcased sustainable city gardens and rain gardens long before these became headline subjects. The Dig In Cookery Theatre hosts chefs and gardeners giving talks and demonstrations, all with the aim of encouraging visitors to grow and cook their own.

There have also been some notable collaborations. In 2017, the RHS and BBC television's *Saturday Kitchen* promoted edible gardens even in the smallest of spaces. This garden, created by award-winning designer Juliet Sargeant, was packed with simple, creative and cost-efficient ways of growing your own in a stylish way. There were small plant pots on shelves next to recipes for herbal teas and stir-fry. There were raised beds with fruits and vegetables, living walls of herbs, and an aquaponics system, with plants receiving nourishment from fish. *Saturday Kitchen* was broadcast from the garden, followed by five episodes of *Kitchen Garden Live* with the Hairy Bikers.

In 2018, the RHS teamed up with the BBC to create *Countryfile*'s '30th Anniversary Garden'. Designed by Ann-Marie Powell, it used 300 different types of plants – over 80 per cent of them native to the British Isles – and included a willow that was over 100 years old. With plenty of ideas on how to encourage wildlife to gardens, it represented different areas of the British Isles, from the Scottish Highlands to the south coast of England, with a nod to the landscape of Ireland.

The show also responds to historical events and anniversaries. In 2017, Andrew Fisher-Tomlin and Dan Bowyer's 'It's All About Community' garden, together with the charity Blind Veterans UK, won a Gold medal and the award for Best Construction. And in 2018,

Opposite: The Floral Marquee is often crammed with visitors – there's not enough room to swing a 'catmint'.

Above: In striped deckchairs and sun hats, the audience take in some live music on the Village Green Bandstand.

Left, top: In 2017 the Blind Veterans UK 'It's All About Community' garden won Gold and Best Construction awards. It featured sinuous, organic, woven-willow sculptures in contrasting dark and pale tones to help visually impaired visitors.

Left, bottom: A traditional display of roses in the Plant Heritage Marquee in 2010.

Left, top: The Cook & Grow Theatre is the place to glean hints and tips from the experts.

Left, bottom: The Long Water at Hampton Court is a perfect place to sit and enjoy the view towards the palace.

Top: Nurseries often experiment with eye-catching ideas to attract visitors and photographers. And it works.

Above: The garden as political statement. In 2017, the 'Not For Sale' conceptual garden raged against the destruction caused by the ivory trade.

'Battlefields to Butterflies' commemorated the twenty-four Royal Parks and Palaces gardeners and park keepers who lost their lives during the First World War. It was created in collaboration with Hampton Court Palace's own gardeners and volunteers.

Each year, the best show gardens and exhibits are awarded the coveted Tudor Rose Award. Barbara Hunt won one of her several Tudor Rose Awards in 1993 with 'Square Roots' – a garden that was largely built with reclaimed and recycled materials. Matthew Soper of Hampshire Carnivorous Plants has won the Tudor Rose three times.

In order to satisfy the demands of the plant buying public, the floral marquee was expanded in 2010. It now spans 6,750 square metres/72,656 square feet and is equivalent in length to almost two football pitches. In 2014, it hosted ninety-five nurseries, seven of which have exhibited every year since the first show in 1990: Blackmore & Langdon, The Botanic Nursery, Fibrex Nurseries, Hardy's Cottage Garden Plants, Southfield Nursery, Squires Garden Centre and W.S. Warmenhoven.

On the twenty-fifth anniversary in 2015, show gardens included 'A Music Lover's Garden' featuring an outdoor performing space, and 'Henri Le Worm', a community garden with its own outdoor kitchen. Historic-themed designs included a garden from Amnesty International, celebrating 800 years since the Magna Carta, and there was a giant, 4-metre/13-foot birthday cake made of begonias to mark the occasion.

The year 2019 signals a change in direction, and the RHS Hampton Court Palace Garden Festival promises to live up to its new name. The popular and much loved show gardens and floral marquee remain, with the addition of more walkthrough garden experiences, 'have a go' activities, music, and, above all, the atmosphere of a giant garden party.

# RHS Flower Show Tatton Park

For five days in late July, 11 hectares/28 acres of deer park is transformed into the RHS show at Tatton Park. Reflecting fashionable Cheshire, it has been a byword for stylish show gardens and boutique shopping since its inception. It also strives to reflect the history and character of the north-west in the Back-to-Back Gardens, displays of fruit and vegetables and its sense of community, friendship and fun. In 2014, Poet Laureate Carol Ann Duffy performed one of her poems in a spectacular show garden designed by her friend Joan Mulvenna. Celebrity guests included comedian Ken Dodd, who opened a flower bed designed by Preston Council, in honour of his comic roots.

Style and success are certainly ingredients of this event. The Talks Theatre has featured interviews with broadcaster Ellie Harrison of BBC's *Countryfile* and BBC newscaster Louise Minchin, who has a long association with the show. Catwalk fashion shows celebrate the talents of final-year students from Manchester School of Art, with models flaunting degree-show designs. At the grand finale in 2011, a new jewellery collection was presented by design icon and keen gardener Zandra Rhodes.

The Flower School Marquee provides great photo opportunities, and in 2010 it hosted the prestigious Eurofleurs competition. Dubbed the Eurovision of floristry, it wowed visitors with displays by some of Europe's most creative young floral artists. In 2018, on the show's twentieth anniversary, visitors voted for their favourite 'Flower Tower'. These had been skilfully decorated by local students, designers, businesses and communities using cut flowers, fir cones and even origami butterflies. Under the tutelage of floral artist Dennis van Wonderen, there were workshops allowing visitors to plant up their own 'on trend' terrarium or create a beautiful crown to take home.

Youthful design is also highlighted in the RHS Young Designer of the Year, a competition created to nurture young garden designers. Each designer is given a budget by the RHS to build a garden and, since 2014, they have been mentored by experienced designer Paul Hervey-Brookes. In 2010, the winner of the RHS Young Designer of the Year Award and Best Show Garden was Hugo Bugg for 'The Albert Dock'. His practice has since won Gold medals at Chelsea, and designed the kitchen garden at RHS Garden Bridgewater (see pages 236–9).

'Young Designer' gardens also reflect RHS campaigns and causes. Ula Maria won in 2017 with her concept for 'Studio Unwired' – a contemporary outdoor hot-desk office for an urban setting, reflecting the impact of gardens on wellbeing. In 2018, Young Designer of the Year and Gold medallist Will Williams' garden, 'At One', reflected the ethos of the RHS Plants for Pollinators campaign. His light, airy contemporary style garden featured a hornbeam hedge providing shelter for wildlife, and he used pollinator-friendly plants, where bees, butterflies and insects would flourish. It was full of take-home tips for visitors, showing how to create a beautiful garden to be enjoyed by both people and wildlife.

Twelve Back-to-Back gardens featured at the first show and, apart from a short break between 2012 and 2015, they have remained a constant feature. Briony Doubleday's 2018 garden 'The Penumbra', in support of the Stroke Association, swept the board with an RHS Gold medal and three other awards: Best Back-to-Back Garden, Best Construction and People's Choice. Featuring tree ferns, corten steel and rusting scaffolding poles, with planting schemes in tones of soft yellow and apricot, it showed visitors how lush, verdant planting can thrive in shade.

James Youd secured Gold in 2018 with a traditional design in his cameo of the gardens at Arley Hall, one of Cheshire's Gardens of Distinction. His double herbaceous borders were a rich mix of intense blue, purple and burgundy flanking a narrow brick path with a bespoke garden gate at the end. Ideal for demonstrating big ideas for small spaces, the Back-to-Back gardens have also been filled with plenty of take-home ideas for visitors, inspiring them to grow plants and proving it is possible to make the most of the smallest urban space.

Tatton is renowned as a show for avant-garde expression and innovation. In 2010, in the Visionary Gardens category, Tony Smith created 'A Matter of Time'. Visitors were somewhat bemused by a shallow crater set in a rectangular framework of black 'scorched' grass, densely planted with bright green oak-leaf lettuce. In the centre of the hollow lay a silver-grey alien surrounded by a circle of red lettuce. It mooted the idea that alien encounters may or may not just be a matter of time, but also of space. It was not the only challenging installation that year. Tony Heywood's 'Space Ritual' incorporated performance art with a shaman-style ritual involving yeti-like creatures raking gravel. That year, the plight of Rwandan refugees, the role of women in society and the ongoing battle with HIV were also portrayed, highlighting the fact that show gardens can be a way to air serious issues.

In a bid to promote and retain traditional skills of the north, local authorities and community groups relish the opportunity to demonstrate their prowess in the National Flower Bed Competition. Although many opt for old-school formal planting or carpet bedding, one of four Gold medals awarded in 2011 was for a memorable design created by Chris Evans and David Ifould of Bournemouth Borough Council. Entitled 'A Novel Approach', it represented the dark world of fictional characters such as Dr Jekyll and Mr Hyde or Frankenstein. The bed was divided into two: on one side, silver planting overarched by a wicker angel symbolised heaven; on the other, fiery coleus, cannas, rudbeckias and dahlias portrayed its terrifying opposite – hell.

School gardens, first featured in 2005, remain essential viewing. What began as a single garden, created by Oakfield Special School and planted by the pupils in the Back-to-Back category, became three the following year. Now, around twenty schools take part in their own School Gardens category each year.

The Green Fields, introduced in 2018, is a colourful, fun-filled area devoted entirely to entertaining and educating children. Here, the School Gardens category took on an artist-inspired theme, reflecting the style of well-known painters such as Pablo Picasso, Salvador Dali and Claude Monet. With pebbles painted as bees, planters made from recycled milk cartons and paving created from bottles, there was a wealth of ideas to delight and enthral visitors.

In the National Plant Societies and Plant Heritage Marquee, displays of fascinating plant collections are put together by specialist groups. Miniature orchids, alpines from around the world and firework-like chrysanthemums sit alongside more familiar cottage garden plants, creatively arranged vegetables and highly scented sweet peas.

There is always a strong northern bias to the nurseries found in the Floral Marquee, and exhibitors include Harperley Hall Farm Nurseries from County Durham; Tinnisburn Plants from Dumfries and Galloway; and Bluebell Cottage Nursery, based near Warrington. Visitors are always attracted to the fabulous displays of fruit and vegetables in the Grow Your Own Marquee.

Left, top: Over the years the female prisoners at HMP & YOI Styal have designed and built several attractive, thought-provoking gardens at Tatton Park Show.

Left, bottom: Pip Probert used frames to divide the garden into rooms in 'Through the Looking Glass' in 2016.

Right, top: Bruntwood, a headline sponsor at Tatton, also encourage young garden designers. In 2017, 'The Bruntwood Experiment', designed by Planit-IE, was based on the Japanese art of kokedama.

Right, bottom: Will Williams won RHS Young Designer of the Year in 2018, the tenth anniversary of the competition, for his design 'At One', a garden where people and nature could live in harmony.

Left, top: The team from Cabasa Carnival Arts injected all their enthusiasm into their bus stop makeover 'Jungle is Massive', celebrating the tropical rainforests in Brazil and the Caribbean and their cultures, people and carnivals.

Left, bottom: Bus Stop Boulevard in 2017 showed a whole range of ideas and elements of nostalgia.

Below: Nursery owners can now win an award for innovative design.

Right: Drone photography offers a completely different perspective of the show.

'Where else could you find an ex-RAF Lightning pilot, a school governor and a story-telling Druid, all talking about their passion for bees?'

Over the years, prisoners from HMP Styal have created many show gardens, seeking to improve themselves through gardening. For some, it is the first time they have tried their hand at horticulture, while others use it as experience to gain further qualifications. Creating a show garden helps them develop new skills, and build a sense of pride and community spirit, which in turn builds self-esteem and confidence. In 2015, a garden named 'Picking up the Pieces' demonstrated the prisoners' desire to move forward in their lives and inspire others going through difficult times. In 2016, the 'Pulling Back Time' garden urged visitors to reflect and take time to focus on what is important in life, and used the positive message to reflect on darker times in their own lives. In 2017 'Stop, Think, Change' was designed by women who had been positively influenced by the probation service's Thinking Skills Programme.

Ideas are constantly being introduced or adapted. One year a butterfly dome came to Tatton, filled with tropical plants and butterflies, and in 2018 bees buzzed in the Bee Hive – a large dome that hosted workshops and demonstrations. Where else could you find an ex-RAF Lightning pilot, a school governor and a story-telling Druid, all talking about their passion for bees?

The RHS Flower Show Tatton Park celebrates the traditions and glamour of the north of England, people's passion for plants, and pride in their heritage. More importantly, it is a show where everyone feels they are among like-minded people who are gathering for a great day out to celebrate gardening.

Left: Cardiff was the first city in the UK to twin with a city in China, a fact celebrated by the 'China Tea' garden, designed by Sue Thomas in 2014.

Right: Scamp's Daffodils' immaculately presented display is always an uplifting sight.

# RHS Flower Show Cardiff

The RHS Flower Show Cardiff – held in Bute Park since 2005 – was the first RHS show to be hosted outside England. It is the first of the outdoor season and is extremely popular with gardeners desperately seeking early signs of spring. Conveniently placed on the edge of Cardiff city centre, this homely show attracts people from all over Britain and is notable for the large number of visitors to its temporary showground.

Welsh horticultural heritage is the focus of the show, but there is also a strong family ethos. One of the highlights is the wheelbarrow competition, which was launched in 2014 in collaboration with Bute Park Education Centre and the RHS Campaign for School Gardening. Pre-schools and schools of the local area are invited to create themed gardens in the smallest of plots: a compost-filled wheelbarrow. Each year they dream up fantastic imaginings of the show theme, with the prizes awarded by public vote.

Show gardens have been at the heart of the Cardiff show since its inception, although they have to be constructed without excavation as the park is on an historical site. The subjects change annually and champion Welsh themes such as myths and legends in 2017, the sea in 2018, and discovery in 2019, as well as reflecting the charitable work and aims of the RHS.

In 2016, the life of author and Cardiff resident Roald Dahl was celebrated in Tony Smith's 'Pure Imagination' garden. It magnificently recreated the pool of chocolate and candy from Willy Wonka's chocolate factory. Dried seed heads and cut flowers were presented in a chocolate-box selection of colours with a spectacular chocolate lake centrepiece bubbling away, filling the air with the delicious aroma of cocoa.

In the same year, Melinda Thomas and Fleur Porter won the Gold and Best in Show for their garden 'Hiraeth'. It contained elements of ruined buildings, mimicking those found scattered around the Welsh countryside, set in patches of semi-woodland.

In 2017, Chris Myers was inspired by the *Mabinogion*, a book of Welsh legends that told the story of Blodeuwedd, a woman created from flowers. His woodland and water garden was crafted to recreate a naturalistic landscape.

Some of the designers who have created gardens at Cardiff have gone on to achieve fame elsewhere. Authors and TV presenters the Rich Brothers first came to Cardiff in 2012 with their garden 'Naturalistic', which focused on using sustainable materials in the garden. Following this, they won Gold at Chelsea in 2013 and 2015. In 2012, multiple Chelsea Gold medal winner Chris Beardshaw, supported by Groundwork, the RHS and M&S, designed 'Urban Oases' at Cardiff and at every other RHS show of that year. It was the first time a designer had exhibited at all the RHS shows in one season.

An exciting new show category called Regeneration Gardens was launched in 2018 to support newly qualified garden designers. Funded by the RHS and mentored by Melinda Thomas, their aim was to show that it is possible to garden sustainably while still crafting beautiful spaces. In 2018, Millie Souter won Best Show Garden and Best Construction for her design using an up-cycled water tank she discovered while out walking in Scotland. Pam Creed's garden, 'The Reimagined Past', used paving, walls and garden furniture constructed from materials discarded from homes being modernised. The National Museum of Wales created three 'mini laboratories' to showcase the regenerative power of nature

and it won the Best Show Feature Award. Meanwhile, the 'RHS Grow Together Garden' presented ideas of how the RHS could collaborate with families and communities.

As well as the show gardens, a host of specialist plant nurseries exhibit in two marquees here. As Cardiff is the earliest RHS show of the year, it is often the first chance that gardeners have to buy something new for their gardens and, as a result, it is one of the most popular shows for buying plants.

Among the nursery exhibits, the show-stopping displays of Ron Scamp's Quality Daffodils are always a highlight. Visitors are amazed by the beauty and variety of so many different daffodils – the Welsh national flower – simply displayed in green vases against a dark baize background and bordered with contrasting leaves of cherry laurel. Each exhibit contains around 175 varieties selected from all thirteen Divisions, including species, historical and modern hybrid cultivars. Exhibiting for the past twelve years, this nursery has been awarded a Gold medal every year and Best in the Floral Marquee ten times (only five nurseries have ever won this prestigious award at Cardiff). At the 2019 Cardiff show, Ron Scamp was rightly honoured as an RHS Master Grower.

Family-run nursery Pheasant Acre Plants, from Bridgend in South Wales, are renowned for their displays of gladioli. At this spring show, however, they turn their attention to tulips and other early bulbs. Their regular displays, a vibrant array of scent and colour, announce the arrival of spring and always create a welcome buzz among visitors.

During your visit, you might find gardening heroes, like champion chrysanthemum grower Ivor Mace or radio personality,

'Conveniently placed on the edge of Cardiff city centre, this homely show attracts people from all over Britain and is notable for the large number of visitors to its temporary showground.'

author and broadcaster Terry Walton, from BBC Radio 2's *Jeremy Vine Show*, chatting with local gardeners and growers. The intimate and friendly RHS Cardiff Flower Show truly reflects the proud Welsh horticultural heritage, both in the flowers and garden designs on display and in the passion for horticulture shown by its visitors and growers – all united by the RHS and a collective love of gardening.

Left: In 2014, designers Andrew Fisher-Tomlin and Dan Bowyer won Best in Show and RHS Gold for their woodland garden, which remained in Bute Park after the show.

Below: Proctor's Nursery chose a traditional style for their stand in the Plant Village in 2018.

Above: A rugby ball in the centre of Rhydypenau Primary School's entry in the Schools Wheelbarrow Competition in 2013 shows exactly where their allegiance lies.

Right, top: Pheasant Acre Plants is always popular with visitors, who are eager to support a top Welsh nursery.

Right: Ottershaw Cacti display a wide range of cacti and succulents of all shapes and forms.

Left: Guess who's running the show?

Right: The Living Laboratory encouraged people to stop, look and learn.

# RHS Chatsworth Flower Show

The preview day for the very first RHS Chatsworth Flower Show – held on the Chatsworth estate in Derbyshire on 6 June 2017 – was battered by gale-force winds and lashing rain, resulting in the showground being closed for safety reasons. The gardening public was not to be deterred, however, as busy roads around the estate proved when the show re-opened to visitors in the days that followed.

The Chatsworth estate not only provided the RHS with a spectacular setting for a new show catering to gardeners in the region, but it seemed particularly appropriate as it celebrated the legacy of three important figures in gardening history: Lancelot 'Capability' Brown, John Wedgwood of Wedgwood Pottery and Sir Joseph Paxton.

'Capability' Brown redesigned the landscape of the estate for the 4th Duke of Devonshire between the late 1750s and 1765. John Wedgwood was a founding member of the Horticultural Society of London, which later became the Royal Horticultural Society, and his father Josiah had presented the Duchess of Devonshire with a set of decorative flower pots in 1778. Paxton was a student gardener at the Horticultural Society's first experimental gardens in Chiswick before becoming head gardener at Chatsworth in 1826, and later designed the Great Conservatory, which was completed in 1840.

In respect to their legacy, the ethos of the RHS Chatsworth Show is to marry the old with the new, champion the innovative and create an event that is playful, fun and unforgettable. To this end, the theme of the first show was 'Design Revolutionaries', and a new category was introduced to allow garden designers freedom of expression and an opportunity to celebrate the connection between plants, sculpture, art and people.

The centrepiece for the 2017 show was a striking 14-metre/46-foot inflatable replica of Joseph Paxton's Great Conservatory, which was filled with exotic plants, including forty large architectural trees and palms, more than 5,000 tropical plants, and hundreds of banana plants – all arranged by Chatsworth's gardeners.

Other attractions included the 'Rhubarb Farm', a 1940s wartime garden filled with fruit and vegetables, many bug hotels created by local schools, and eight gardens in the Freeform category. Among the show gardens, the 'IQ Quarry Garden' by Paul Hervey-Brookes won Best in Show. Its concept was based around the lifecycle of a quarry, focusing on the flora and habitats found in quarries before and after they are excavated.

A constant source of excitement was the Palladian-style bridge decorated by celebrated local floral designer Jonathan Moseley. Classical in appearance on the outside, it led visitors through a tunnel adorned in an explosion of contemporary floral flamboyance, and a gigantic wickerwork snake rose from the water and threaded its way through the structure. Waxy-textured plants and flowers covered the snake's body like scaly skin, with the colours becoming increasingly vibrant and fiery as they reached its head.

In 2018, the weather was much kinder than in the previous year. Chatsworth House's long historical connection with orchids was reflected in the inflatable Great Conservatory, which made a reappearance and was this time filled with over 7,000 *Phalaenopsis* orchids from one hundred different varieties. It was a full-on moth orchid extravaganza – again the work of florist Jonathan

Moseley. Elsewhere, the RHS supported local floral designers with an opportunity to showcase their talents by creating a floral installation inspired by the drama and opulence of couture fashion through history.

A spectacular river of 12,000 *Cosmos bipinnatus* 'Razzmatazz Pink' provided visitors with a dramatic sight at the entrance to the show, with iconic Chatsworth House in the background. A new Long Border Competition took inspiration from the borders of great places such as Chatsworth, Haddon Hall, and RHS Garden Wisley. It featured eight raised beds on the theme of movement, with plenty of take-home planting ideas for visitors. Louisa van den Berg's border, 'Mind the Gap: Bees on the Move', reflected the Plants for Pollinators campaign. Voted Best in Show, it featured wickerwork bees and a skep surrounded by bee-friendly plants like alliums, lupins and borage that flower in June, when there is often a gap in the nectar supply.

Another new feature was the RHS Living Laboratory, which explored the vital role plants play within a city. A food zone here demonstrated how to grow crops in small spaces, and displays explained how plants help prevent flooding, and how their leaves trap pollutants. A green room with living walls and the sound of birdsong was an example of how plants and gardening encourage a sense of wellbeing, while another area demonstrated how gardening is good exercise for the body as well as the mind. There were even hydroponically grown salads for visitors to nibble at the exit.

Phil Hurst scooped the Best Show Garden award for 'The Great Outdoors' – his celebration of the local environment. With a water feature flowing through the centre, this garden and its planting reflected the beauty of the surrounding moors, peat bogs and woodlands. The People's Choice Garden was Chris Myers' 'Haytime in the Dales'; this also took the northern landscape as its inspiration.

In a community area next to the show gardens, visitors found competition entries from community gardening groups, including Britain in Bloom and RHS Affiliated Societies, alongside up-cycled planters filled with colourful blooms from schools that participate in the RHS Campaign for School Gardening.

Once a year, the glorious architecture of Chatsworth House and its beautiful landscape formed by expansive parkland, the winding River Derwent and a natural backdrop of wooded hills, provide a wonderful location for everyone to celebrate the joys of gardening. The RHS Chatsworth Flower Show, now entering its third year, holds plenty of promise as a new show with fresh ideas, including a wealth of displays highlighting important contemporary issues and current RHS campaigns. It's an exciting day out and underpinning it all there is an underlying message about the importance of gardening and plants.

Left, top: The Great Conservatory made its first appearance at Chatsworth in 1840; the second at the RHS show in 2017.

Left, bottom: In 2017, designer Jo Thompson won the People's Choice Award for her show garden by the river in the new Freeform category.

Below: Dancers, frozen in time on Press Day 2018, at the Brewin Dolphin Installation designed by Paul Hervey-Brookes.

Right, top: The 2017 Wedgwood Garden – 'A Classic Re-imagined' – by Sam Ovens was notable for its beautiful planting and stonework.

Right, bottom: Contemporary buildings and traditional plants make a pleasing combination.

# RHS garden flower shows

After careful consideration, the RHS shifted its focus away from London events towards its shows at RHS gardens around the country, where they believed they would attract more visitors, inspire more people to grow plants, and help specialist nurseries to flourish. The decision was vindicated by the increase in visitor numbers: more than 45,000 people now attend the annual shows at Wisley; 29,000 at Hyde Hall; nearly 14,000 at Harlow Carr; and over 9,000 at Rosemoor. The garden flower shows have also become an incentive for members to make their first visit to RHS gardens further afield.

The focus at each show is on bringing together a large number of nurseries from all over Britain into one place and promoting local nurseries. They are a wonderful opportunity for visitors to buy plants from specialist suppliers, which might be challenging for them to visit individually, while at the same time enjoying a great day out.

The events teams from all the gardens meet every year to select the nurseries they will invite, with the final selections approved by a panel made up of RHS Council members and judges. This process ensures that the quality of the shows remains consistently high, since there are a large number of applicants for each plant category, and it also means a good variety of plant growers is guaranteed. For example, the summer shows are heavily oversubscribed by nurseries selling herbaceous plants, so applications from other plant groups need to be encouraged. The selection process also encourages new nurseries to apply, with eight new nurseries appearing in 2019.

What started as a three-day show at RHS Garden Hyde Hall in late July 2010 is now a five-day floral extravaganza, sited around the Clover Hill and Road Field areas of the garden. This joyful celebration of plants and gardening has become incredibly popular. In the first year, 7,600 people visited the show; by 2017 over 5,000 on average were appearing on every single day.

Forty specialist nurseries attend the show at Hyde Hall. The nurseries here offer plants from twenty-three different groups, from *Acer* to *Mandevilla*, and from carnivorous plants to succulents. As well as the plant sales, there are plenty of opportunities to buy gardening sundries, tools and equipment, and even garden furniture. Visitors can talk to RHS advisers for some expert gardening advice, relax to the sound of live music from marching bands, jazz ensembles and harpists in a covered seating area near the lake, and enjoy a wide selection of delicious food and drink. It is also a marvellous opportunity to explore the garden in full summer bloom.

The RHS Garden Rosemoor Flower Show, first held in 2017, takes place over a weekend in mid-August, at a time of year when the garden and holiday season are in full swing in Devon. For ease of access, visitors can park for free in Torrington town centre and take a shuttle bus – all part of a great family day out. This intimate and informal show is centred on the Fruit Field and around the lake, where nurseries showcase their plants in 'mini' show gardens in front of their stands. The twenty-three nurseries from near and far sell a wide range of plants, including many that are choice and hard to find. It is the ideal place to pick up a longed-for addition to your garden.

The layout at the Rosemoor show and the nurseries that appear there are all chosen so that local RHS members can experience the atmosphere and excitement of one of the larger RHS shows, albeit on a much smaller scale. Local bands play a range of music that floats over the lake, creating a relaxing, fun-filled atmosphere. Nurseries are joined by trade stands and there are talks and demonstrations given

181

> 'The focus at each show is on bringing together a large number of nurseries from all over Britain into one place and promoting local nurseries.'

Left, top: Architectural alliums are always eye-catching in baskets, beds or borders.

Left, bottom: There is always an impressive array of vegetables on show at the Taste of Autumn Festival at Wisley.

Above: After looking at such a wonderful display of skill, it is not surprising so many people want to be a floral artist.

by garden staff, RHS advisers and owners of specialist nurseries. There is also entertainment for children. In the past, this has included circus skills drop-in sessions, where children are taught juggling and other tricks, and a hands-on musical instrument area.

Visitors can also take time to explore the gardens. In 2018, the garden shelters were transformed by the North Devon Flower Clubs and members of the National Association of Flower Arranging Societies (NAFAS), each one having a Beatrix Potter theme. Members of both clubs gave flower arranging demonstrations daily during the show. Floral designer Jonathan Moseley's British Flower Bus was an added attraction; well known for his role on the BBC's *The Big Allotment Challenge*, Jonathan gave two flower arranging demonstrations each day while championing British-grown flowers.

There is always a sprinkling of stardust at the six-day RHS Garden Wisley Flower Show, which started in 1992 and is held during the first week in September. In 2014, TV cook Mary Berry helped to open the show by adding a final rose to the three-tiered cake display made by floral decorator Simon Lycett. She returned again in 2015 to take a large slice from a giant Victoria sponge cake made of flowers to celebrate the show's opening. In 2018, the show was opened by much-loved star of stage and screen – and keen gardener – Dame Judi Dench.

The Wisley show is spread throughout Seven Acres, the Glasshouse and the Wilson's Wood area. The relaxed atmosphere is enhanced by extra seating placed around the gardens, inviting visitors to take time out from buying plants and sit back and enjoy 'the best in horticulture'.

There is always an undercurrent of excitement around the fifty-five nursery stands at Wisley's show. It is held during bulb planting

Above: All stocked up and ready to go at Wisley Flower Show. Now for the customers.

Right, top: The Wisley Flower Show hosts the National Dahlia Society Annual Show, an exciting 'extra' for visitors.

Right, centre: Harlow Carr Autumn Plant Fair often features a fine display of local apples. Advice on suitable selections is always welcomed by gardeners.

Right, bottom: Hyde Hall Autumn Plant Fair is perfectly timed for the bulb-planting season.

time, so there are usually several exhibitors selling bulbs as well as displays from nurseries offering summer herbaceous perennials, which can be relied on to look spectacular. Many of the nurseries are regulars at the main RHS shows, but the society also supports local nurseries like Ottershaw Cacti, who are based near Wisley.

An added treat for visitors is the National Dahlia Society Annual Show, which takes place at the same time. Over one hundred exhibitors compete with one another among thousands of vibrantly coloured blooms. There is a People's Competition for members of the public to submit a dahlia, and there was also a one-off dark foliage dahlia display. Surrey NAFAS are there too, holding their annual floral competition, filled with exquisite creations. Every year, there is a different theme to the event. In 2018 it was 'Something in the Air' and the Glasshouse Gallery displayed the flamboyant floral artwork of Devon artist Anita Nowinska, with many of the paintings inspired by flowers and planting at Wisley.

One aim of the show is to make everything as easy and enjoyable as possible for visitors and exhibitors. Chrissie Milton, Wisley's events manager, once practised wheeling cardboard dahlias in pots from the car park along the route to the dahlia tent just to make sure the path was smooth enough for the real blooms. It's this kind of attention to detail that makes every show a success.

The first three-day show at RHS Garden Harlow Carr was held at the end of June in 2016. The show is focused on the main lawns, but it is also spread throughout the garden because of a shortage of flat ground. The stands are laid out so that people can meander through the garden, encouraging them to explore, and there is still space for those who want to hide away from the crowds. There are over forty-five

specialist plant nurseries, as well as garden trade stands, live music, talks, demonstrations, art exhibitions, a plant crèche and catering from the legendary Betty's Tearooms. Children can enjoy workshops run by the education and communities team. As at Rosemoor, a park-and-ride service from nearby Harrogate eases traffic congestion, freeing up spaces on site for disabled visitors, and adding to the feel of a family day out.

Visitor numbers are up at the four garden shows, and customer satisfaction is high. Each year the shows are reviewed, with new nurseries and events added for visitors to enjoy, but all naturally revolve around excellence in horticulture and plants. Part of the RHS vision is 'to delight our customers with exceptional service and products' and to inspire people to garden. The garden shows do this very well.

The Main Borders at their peak simply glow in the soft light of a glorious summer evening.

# Harlow Carr

## NORTH YORKSHIRE GARDEN

Harlow Carr, the RHS's 23.5-hectare/58-acre Yorkshire garden, owes its existence to the mineral springs of Harrogate, which were first discovered in 1571. The Harlow Carr estate was considered to possess a particularly efficacious spring, so the owner, Henry Wright, built a hotel and bath house in 1844 and laid out pleasure gardens for visitors. The success of his spa and the arrival of the railway in 1848 contributed to the development of Harrogate as an elegant spa town, which thrived until its popularity declined after the First World War.

The Northern Horticultural Society (NHS) sought a northern counterpart to the RHS's experimental garden at Wisley, where 'new plants can be tested for hardiness and suitability to inland climatic conditions north of the Trent', according to the RHS *Journal*. It settled on the remnants of Wright's estate, leasing 12 hectares/30 acres of woodland, rough pasture, a dilapidated bath house and stables: plant trials began in 1949 and Harlow Carr Botanical Gardens opened to the public in 1950.

The original design, created by the NHS's chairman, Colonel Charles Grey, was dominated by straight lines and military precision. A rock garden was built, and woodland cleared and planted with a range of rhododendrons, but further progress was hampered through lack of funds. Gardeners happened to unearth a stash of lead piping, the sale of which paid for the conifer shelter belt north-west of the Arboretum (itself financed by a whip-round among society members). Donations from commercial growers were also a vital source of plants.

Harlow Carr's superintendent Geoffrey Smith raised the profile of the garden when he became a presenter on BBC's *Gardening Club* in the 1950s. This attracted more members to the NHS, but it was not enough to resolve the financial constraints. New possibilities finally opened up when the NHS merged with the RHS in 2001.

Since then, the garden has seen many exciting additions and improvements, including a Winter Walk, Alpine Zone, Learning Centre and a revamped Kitchen Garden. Gardens Through Time, a set of historic gardens created for a 2004 BBC series of the same name, are now being replanted and replaced.

As the NHS first discovered, this is an ideal location for testing plant hardiness. Set in a valley at 155 metres/508 feet above sea level, with temperatures ranging from −13°C /8.6°F to 30°C /86°F, the growing season is short and cool. Winter brings frequent deep frosts, with associated frost pockets and drying winds. An annual rainfall of over 110 centimetres/44 inches a year has in the past caused regular problems with flash flooding and erosion along the stream, but these are now being resolved by the creation of balancing pools, which store excess rainwater. The soil is primarily a heavy, acidic clay and poorly drained in parts (the Norse word *carr* means 'land reclaimed from a bog'). Gardeners at Harlow Carr are pushing the boundaries on behalf of northern gardeners, experimenting with plants to test their hardiness and increase the range found growing in the garden. Dogwoods (*Cornus*) of various sizes have been planted in the woodland to test their hardiness at different stages of growth, along with *Cercidiphyllum japonicum* cultivars; birches (*Betula*), deciduous azaleas (*Rhododendron*), magnolias and rhododendrons, as well as bulbs and herbaceous

plants have been planted here. Not all plants thrive in these conditions, but the upside is that flowers last longer than they do further south.

The Streamside Garden, running the length of Harlow Carr and blending with the woodland beyond, is one of the longest in Britain and home to a vibrant display of colourful, moisture-loving plants. Late spring brings yellow spathes of the (invasive) skunk cabbage (*Lysichiton americanus*), followed by lush, leafy rodgersias, darmeras, hostas, ferns and giant gunneras. There are also large block plantings of irises and astilbes; candelabra primulas have been so successful that the garden even has its own strain, the *Primula* Harlow Carr hybrids, in pink, peach, orange, yellow and purple. Himalayan blue poppies (*Meconopsis*), the legacy of an RHS plant trial held between 2010 and 2013, are also used to great effect and have become one of the garden's signature plants.

Another much-visited feature is the impressive 24-metre/79-foot Alpine House, which opened in May 2009. Maintained by staff and enthusiastic volunteers from the local group of the Alpine Garden Society, it contains over 2,000 different plants set against a backdrop of natural sandstone rock. Landscaped in the style of an alpine habitat, it is punctuated by *Pinus parviflora* 'Gyok-kasen', dwarf rhododendrons and 2.4-metre/8-foot stone monoliths. Plants are grouped according to altitude, with high-alpine cushion plants sited on the highest areas for better air circulation, while plants needing dry habitats are planted directly into sharp sand in the plunge beds to ensure perfect drainage.

There are plans to replace some of the plunge beds with a beginners' corner, with interpretation explaining all about the plants and how to grow them. Staff in all departments are encouraged to chat to visitors and answer their questions, to enhance their visit and help them to enjoy their own gardens even more. External landscaping around the glasshouse is being developed in phases with a series of raised drystone beds, large stone spheres, recycled limestone and tufa and large crevice plantings, complementing the existing landscape. By recycling limestone, the RHS can demonstrate both the importance of habitat conservation and the variety of alpine plants supported by the particular geology and landscape of the Yorkshire Dales.

Fruit and vegetable growing has a long history in RHS gardens, with the RHS 'Grow Your Own' advice service offering extra encouragement and information. Success depends on the soil, and the Kitchen Garden at Harlow Carr demonstrates what can be grown on a windy site with clay soil, using plants that thrive in northern gardens.

Gardening in raised beds (made from recycled plastic milk bottles) avoids the challenges of clay as they warm up faster in spring and are easier for covering or cloching; bark paths around them allow year-round access. The soil in the raised beds is improved annually with the addition of garden compost, rotted manure and mushroom compost, depending on what is to be grown. Crops are sown in succession on a three-year rotation and sowing and harvesting is carefully planned to make the most efficient use of the space and avoid gluts. Flowers and herbs are used as companion plants to attract beneficial insects and deter pests, along with edible flowers like violets, marigolds and nasturtiums, creating a vibrantly coloured mixed planting. An ornamental and edible 3 x 3 metre/10 x 10 foot plot shows how to optimise production in an urban garden.

Left: There are always flowers indoors, or out. A drift of fragrant *Narcissus* 'Sir Winston Churchill' welcomes visitors early in the growing season. What's in the glasshouse? You will have to visit to find out.

Above: A cheerful selection of easy-to-grow sunflowers brings both height and colour to the Kitchen Garden.

Right: The Main Borders at Harlow Carr add a splash of colour to the many tones of green revealed in the surrounding landscape.

Below: Raised beds of alpines demonstrate a simple yet effective way of displaying these tiny plants to their best advantage at home.

Vegetable trials are often informal; if a particular group is being trialled at Wisley, gardeners at Harlow Carr will grow some of the AGM selections for comparison. Not all vegetables are successful. Inspired by Hyde Hall's success at growing giant pumpkins, staff tried one of their own, but it only reached the size of a beach ball. They did however achieve greater success with giant leeks donated by the National Vegetable Society.

A new unheated glasshouse is used mainly in the summer for tender crops like tomatoes, peppers, aubergines, basil and lemongrass, and to provide protection from the weather in the cooler months for hardy salad crops. During the 'Grow Your Own' Autumn Festival, the glasshouse is used for displays of pumpkins as well as for seed and herb drying, and an outdoor oven reminds visitors of the direct link between the crops and the kitchen, the benefits of zero 'food miles' and the improved quality and flavour of crops picked at their peak.

The Main Borders have been renovated and altered several times, most recently in 2005, retaining the mature specimen trees from the original planting. The modern prairie-style design combines herbaceous perennials and grasses in bold, complementary drifts, planted relatively close together, providing natural plant support and inspirational associations. Halfway down the Main Borders is an informal roundel planted with hardy geraniums, molinias, perovskias, hundreds of camassias, and six different species of allium appearing in a pattern repeated through all the beds.

The Bramall Learning Centre, completed in 2010, was designed to be one of the 'greenest' buildings in the country, to reflect the

'Gardeners at Harlow Carr are pushing the boundaries on behalf of northern gardeners, experimenting with plants to test their hardiness and increase the range found growing in the garden.'

Garden meets woodland with a vibrant display of spring flowers, with mauve-pink *Rhododendron rubiginosum*, primulas, narcissi and hellebores and fresh spring growth.

Visiting RHS gardens gives everyone a chance to experience gardening on a large and dramatic scale and see familiar plants growing together in impressive groups.

## Outdoor studio

Nel Whatmore, artist in residence at Harlow Carr, is often found working outdoors. Painting in natural light, or *en plein air*, was important to the Impressionist artists, such as Claude Monet, who was famously inspired by the collection of waterlilies in his pond. Artists visit RHS gardens for similar reasons, enabling them to experience plants growing in more natural surroundings and for the pleasure of expressing their skills outdoors rather than being constrained by a studio. 'Art is nature and nature is art,' pronounced Spanish artist César Manrique. Artists whose work has been elevated by a visit to an RHS garden, would entirely agree.

Top: In late winter and early spring, evergreen trees and box cones reveal the underlying structure of the garden. It can often go unnoticed when the garden is in full bloom.

Above: Neat lines of blooms in red and yellow come together where the Streamside Garden meets the Main Borders at Harlow Carr.

Right: The view from one end of the Main Borders reveals the Alpine House, yet another 'must see' destination on your tour of the gardens.

garden's ethos of sustainability. It is built from recycled materials and is well insulated, with a sedum roof, and incorporates solar water heating and a ground source heat pump. A teaching garden and wildlife pond have been created nearby. They are all part of the provision for nearly 12,000 children who visit every year, so staff can enthral and inspire the younger generation of ecologists and gardeners and create life-long links with plants and the landscape.

The range of events covering a variety of themes is typical of an RHS garden. In addition to the 'Grow Your Own' event in autumn, there are Budding Gardeners workshops for families, National Gardening Week activities, a Summer Garden Party, the Great Garden Adventure in the school summer holidays and the Magic of Christmas leading up to the festive season. There are practical day workshops for amateur gardeners, themed demonstrations, spring and autumn plant fairs, outdoor theatre events, garden walks and a variety of craft, art and photographic exhibitions throughout the year, alongside sculptures created by artists in residence. Whatever the event, the focus is on using all the resources the garden has to offer and staff are encouraged to propose ideas, so everyone shares in its success.

The garden helps out local organisations, for example by sending plants, spare flower pots and materials to Horticap, a nearby gardening charity, or by lending a hand to the conservation group maintaining woodlands along a footpath that connects Harrogate with Harlow Carr. Staff contribute to community outreach as far afield as Bradford, Leeds and Wakefield, where they have worked with young offenders and schools. In 2017, a local army regiment donated hundreds of worn-out boots. In a collaboration between the RHS outreach team and schools they were decorated and planted. The project was so successful that the boots remained on display for the whole summer.

Professor Nigel Dunnett of Sheffield University has developed a masterplan for the garden that ensures an exciting and constantly evolving future in keeping with its character. The RHS has also bought the old disused Harrogate Arms Hotel and the streamside bathing areas that preceded the construction of the bath house (now the Bath House Gallery). By doing this, the society hopes to restore the connection between the two buildings with a new landscaping scheme and a new activities building will be constructed adjacent to the refurbished Grade II listed building, which will be a garden cafe. With so many plans and projects proposed for the garden, the future looks bright for northern gardeners.

# Chapter 10
# Inspiring everyone to grow

Planting the 'Taking Stock' Community Garden on the Sheerwater Estate in Woking was a combined effort between the RHS horticulture students and residents.

# Inspiring everyone to grow

When the RHS talks about inspiring everyone to grow, they mean everyone. The beginner is included just as much as the keen plant-lover, and the allotment grower as much as the window-box gardener. The RHS provides many forms of advice and much of it is gathered together on its website. Here you can find the answers to your gardening problems, discover what each branch of the society is up to, participate in citizen science surveys, track down the supplier for a particular plant and check what events and partner gardens are available in your area.

In their diversity, RHS publications reflect the varied world of horticulture. There are hefty reference books, helpful growing guides and plenty of ideas for small gardens. Take your pick. The five branches of the RHS library, including the Lindley Library, in London, with its huge collection of books and images, welcomes anyone wanting to browse through a slice of Britain's gardening heritage, find inspiration for their garden, or simply follow their own horticultural interests wherever they may lead.

With such an enormous range of plants available in the nursery trade, and more new varieties introduced every year, it can be difficult to know which to choose. Not all are worth growing. The Award of Garden Merit marks out high-performing plants that have been approved by RHS panels of experts, often after trials.

Sometimes knowledge is best gained through sharing with friends, and the RHS recognises the communal benefits of horticulture by putting gardeners in touch with specialist and affiliated societies according to their needs. The RHS is also actively developing its use of social media as an immediate, responsive way of communicating and as a way to reach new audiences, inspiring them to get involved in gardening.

There is considerable focus on public education in all the RHS gardens, from curriculum-based lessons for schoolchildren to practical gardening skills for adults and exhibitions for families. The aim to create 'world-leading horticulture that inspires people to garden' means that even non-gardeners on a day out to one of the RHS gardens are unwittingly subject to the influence.

Professional horticulture also needs RHS support. Horticulture remains undersubscribed as a career because of the widespread misconception that jobs in horticulture are for the unskilled. This is a longstanding problem, yet garden designers, plantspeople, botanists, curators of scientific collections, landscape consultants, plant pathologists, entomologists, taxonomists and writers all come under the umbrella of horticulture. Skilled horticulturists contribute more to the British economy than has been fully recognised, and their work greatly benefits our health and wellbeing. This was actually, for the first time, rigorously confirmed in a 2018 report commissioned by the Ornamental Horticulture Roundtable Group, a sector-led group chaired by RHS Director General Sue Biggs, which found that ornamental horticulture contributes an estimated £24.2 billion to the UK's GDP. The government has been taking an increasing interest in the social and economic impact of horticulture, and the RHS continues to call for policies that support the industry to prosper and help society more broadly.

The RHS has pledged to encourage more young people to consider horticulture as a career, through its involvement in the Horticulture Matters campaign and its own, highly regarded qualifications and the work-based training programmes offered by the RHS School of Horticulture. RHS bursaries make it possible for horticulturists to travel and gain experience abroad. These are opportunities to seize.

# Compare and contrast

## PLANT TRIALS AND THE AWARD OF GARDEN MERIT

Now and then the RHS plant trials catch the public imagination. In August 2018 BBC *Breakfast* presenter Carol Kirkwood broadcast the weather forecast from the trials ground at RHS Garden Wisley, surrounded by 140 varieties of marigold thriving despite the summer's drought. It was the Year of the Marigold and Wisley's visitors were invited to vote for their favourite flower. The People's Choice award went to lemon yellow 'Alumia Vanilla Cream', revealing a preference for unconventional varieties.

Every year the RHS runs around thirty different plant trials (onions, viburnums and peonies are recent examples), and the People's Choice was introduced in 2014 as a way of getting the public involved. Most trials are planted in the Portsmouth Field at Wisley, but other RHS gardens, partner gardens and nurseries around the UK participate so that plants can be studied under different growing conditions. Hyde Hall has been helping with the trial of coloured-stemmed dogwoods (*Cornus*), while winter cabbages have been put to the test at Rosemoor.

The main purpose of a trial is to grow different selections of the same plant side by side under the same conditions to test their performance. For visitors, they act as a sort of living catalogue and are useful for making comparisons. A small trial has around 50 entries, a large one 200, and all generally include a mixture of new varieties and well-established garden plants. Once a list of names has been fixed for a particular trial, seed companies, national collections, gardens and nurseries are invited to send in the required plants.

Over a set period of time, usually between one and three years, the plants are evaluated by a panel of judges known as a trials forum. The judges often belong to RHS specialist plant committees and are joined by other experts from scientific institutions and the horticultural industry. They visit the plants as often as needed to assess them. It could be every few weeks or twice a year, depending on when the plants flower, fruit or crop. Not every trial runs according to plan, it has to be said: plants in the off-site trial of *Erica* heathers at the Threave Garden in Scotland were initially got at by deer.

When a trial comes to an end, the judging panel decides which plants have out-performed the rest. These are singled out for the Award of Garden Merit (AGM), the highest accolade the RHS can give to a plant. To obtain an AGM, plants must be healthy, resistant to the weather, excellent for garden use and widely available. The awards scheme has been helping gardeners choose outstanding and reliable plants ever since it was established in 1922. Today it covers over 7,500 edible and ornamental plants, which often carry the distinctive green trophy logo in nurseries and garden centres.

Another role of trials is to resolve possible confusion in the horticultural trade over plant naming and identities. Sometimes cultivars that look the same are submitted under several names, or entries with the same name turn out to be different. To avoid problems like this recurring, all AGM-winning plants are photographed, and correctly named samples are preserved as herbarium specimens for future reference.

Plant groups are chosen for trial in a number of ways, often taking account of gardening trends. The RHS flower shows are a good place to spot current tastes, and RHS specialist plant committee members, who

Above: There are chrysanthemums as far as the eye can see on the Trials Field at Wisley.

Left: *Camellia × williamsii* 'Donation' received an AGM in 1993.

Bottom left: Plant portrait of the bushy shrub *Rosa* 'Poulmax' AGM.

Bottom right: When buying for your garden, look out for Plants for Pollinators and the AGM logo.

Right: The trial beds at Wisley in summer are a patchwork of texture and colour, with vibrant annuals, herbaceous plants, shrubs and leafy vegetables. Although ornamental, the Trial Field's primary role is as a living outdoor laboratory, where plants are cultivated and assessed – a vital factor in the success of the AGM.

'To obtain an AGM, plants must
be healthy, resistant to the
weather, excellent for garden
use and widely available.'

are in contact with plant breeders, also bring ideas forward. As an example, shrubby hydrangeas (*Hydrangea macrophylla*) were selected because breeding work in Europe and Japan has led to many new introductions. Which of these plants offer a real improvement on existing cultivars will be revealed by the trial.

The People's Choice award is another barometer of plant fashions. *Begonia* and *Lantana* were popular in 2018 (pink-frilled *Begonia* 'Sweet Spice Bounty Coral' won the most votes) and were each selected to become the subject of a full-scale trial in their own right. The trials programme also looks at environmental issues such as gardening in a changing climate. The current outdoor trial of crape myrtle (*Lagerstroemia*) is a good example. This subtropical shrub is widely used in the United States and Mediterranean regions but until now no one has thought it would perform well outdoors

in the UK throughout the year. The trial is proving that we need to investigate other plants with this potential.

The RHS has recently begun publishing the results of its trials in a handy series of illustrated *Grower Guides*. The first three focus on *Penstemon, Euphorbia* and ornamental alliums, giving cultivation advice and a list of suppliers, as well as insights into why the trial was held and what the forum thought. Special study days at Wisley and other trials sites are open to anyone interested in learning more. Hibiscus and agapanthus were recently in the limelight.

Trials are in fact only part of the story. More than half the current total of AGMs have been awarded following round-table assessments. This is when horticultural experts debate the characteristics and garden performance of plants from their own experience, often because a trial is impractical or impossible for certain plant groups. Hostas, birches and *Brugmansia* (datura) are currently being evaluated in this way.

Since 2013, a rolling programme of reviews carried out by the RHS specialist plant committees ensures that each plant on the AGM list still merits its award. Some varieties are surpassed by better introductions or lose their garden-worthiness over time, so these are withdrawn from the list annually.

As part of the great works underway at Wisley, plant trialling will move from its familiar location beyond Battleston Hill to a more intimate and ornamental Trials Garden on the site of the current plant centre. Anyone curious about the best plants to grow will be making a beeline.

# A global knowledge bank

## LIBRARIES

What started out as a row of books on a shelf at 21 Regent Street (the society's first head office) is now one of the most important collections of botanical art and garden history in Britain, comprising approximately 100,000 books, nearly a quarter of a million photographs and 30,000 artworks. It holds the society's archives and also personal papers of renowned gardeners like William Robinson and E.A. Bowles. The library was an essential day-to-day working tool from the time the first books were acquired in 1806, and remains so, supporting researchers and students in a wide range of subjects, from garden historians in search of early printed books to children needing help with school projects. Staff answer over 16,000 enquiries from RHS members and the public every year.

In addition to the Lindley Library in London, there are garden libraries with reference and loan collections at Wisley and Harlow Carr, and satellite reference libraries at Rosemoor and Hyde Hall. There is also a specialist research library for plant science and horticultural taxonomy at Wisley, where the strategic investment project will see the creation of a brand new library. This will give public access for the first time to both the garden library and research collections, together with better facilities for collection storage and display.

When the society faced serious financial trouble in the late 1850s, the London library, herbarium and art collections were sold, an act that was instantly regretted (although the library in the council room at the Chiswick garden survived and became the core of the research collection at Wisley). In 1865 the society bought the library of orchidologist and former RHS secretary John Lindley, after whom the

Lindley Library is named. The collection was soon expanded by several large bequests and donations, notably that of coal and iron magnate Reginald Cory (1871–1934), an obsessive bibliophile and collector of botanical art; some of the library's most precious items were originally his, such as the pen-and-ink drawings of Claude Aubriet (1665–1742) and an edition of Turpin's *Leçon de Flore* owned by Louis XVIII.

The Lindley Library had various homes until the first purpose-built library, with its own reading room, was opened in 1904 at the society's new Vincent Square headquarters in London. The construction works were financed in part by the orchid-loving Schroeder family, who wanted a hall for showing and a library on site for the study of orchids. Apart from a spell in Wales during the Second World War, this is where the Lindley Library has remained.

Today, the library's archives and photographs offer unparalleled insights into the social history of gardening and are an important part of the UK's cultural heritage, containing a wealth of diaries, correspondence, minutes and plans that are currently being catalogued for the first time. The library also holds a major collection of rare books. The oldest, Pliny's encyclopedic *Historia Naturalis*, dates from 1514, not long after the printing press was invented. There is also a copy of *The Gardener's Labyrinth* (1586) by Thomas Hill, the first gardening manual ever written in English, and a rich selection of original herbals, including texts by John Gerard and Pietro Andrea Mattioli.

The collection of around 200,000 photographs comprises autochromes, glass lantern slides, transparencies and black-and-white prints, including over 700 portrait photographs, mostly of nineteenth-century botanists and gardeners. There are also some very early photographic views from the RHS garden in Kensington (the

society's headquarters 1861–88) taken by Charles Thurston Thompson in 1862.

One of the most interesting Lindley archives is the Ruhleben Collection of photographs and papers. When the First World War broke out, many British civilians in Germany were detained in the Ruhleben internment camp, on the outskirts of Berlin. Overcrowding was a problem, but a lively social life developed and a group of internees ran a garden club affiliated to the RHS (see pages 220–23). The RHS sent them seeds, plants, bulbs, and even instructions on how to run a flower show. They ended up with a better diet than the population of Berlin and many became expert gardeners. (A century later, in April 2018, with the help of the Lemon Tree Trust, the RHS sent a similar shipment of 2,000 packets of vegetable and flower seeds to the Domiz refugee camp in northern Iraq.)

There is a considerable amount of material from the plant collectors who ventured out on behalf of the society, like George Don, David Douglas, Robert Fortune, George Forrest and Carl Theodor Hartweg. The archive contains their field journals, plant lists and correspondence with the society. The Reginald Farrer Collection is unrivalled, preserving letters, paintings, and the glass-lantern slides that he used for lectures on his return. They throw light on the history of plant introductions, and also social history, ethnography and even (in the case of James McRae) mutiny.

The library's extensive collection of nursery catalogues are mainly from British companies of the 1860s onwards, with a few earlier eighteenth-century examples. These are an essential resource for RHS botanists, providing a historical record of cultivated plants. A collection of garden guides documents the changing face of individual gardens, and the collection of over 5,000 postcards of municipal parks is one of only two that are publicly accessible. (The other is held by English Heritage.)

In the late 1890s, RHS President Sir Trevor Lawrence and the newly formed Orchid Committee decided that award-winning orchids should be painted for posterity to a uniform standard, viewed from the front and life-size in scale. The first official orchid artist, 24-year-old Nellie Roberts, was appointed in January 1897 to paint every plant given a First Class Certificate or an Award of Merit. On her retirement almost sixty years later there were a total of 4,500 paintings; now there are around 7,000, all catalogued. As the International Cultivar Registration Authority for orchids (see pages 116–19), the RHS still employs a painter.

The Reeves Collection of Chinese art is another treasure trove, numbering around 790 paintings. They date from the early days of the society, when China was largely closed to Westerners and trade was limited. The eminent scientist Sir Joseph Banks (one of the founders of the RHS) asked his friend John Reeves, a tea agent interested in botany, to send him paintings of the plants he saw in Chinese gardens, along with any information he could find. This Reeves did for around twenty years, employing four artists as servants in his household. They had been trained in Chinese art, but Reeves also taught them how to paint Western botanical illustrations, and the results are an amazing hybrid of the two styles. Through them, Western scientists and gardeners saw plants like wisterias, chrysanthemums and repeat-flowering and yellow roses for the very first time.

The RHS has been making high-resolution digital images of parts of its collections for over fifteen years, in order to licence them for

Left: Lantern slides of the RHS gardens at Kensington c.1875–80. Clockwise from top left: the Royal Albert Hall and statue of Prince Albert beyond; the interior of the conservatory; view of the Great Palm; the statue of St Michael veiled in foliage.

Right: Watercolour on board of flowering x *Brassolaeliocattleya* Midenette by Nellie Roberts, who was appointed by the RHS in 1897 to paint orchids and was awarded the Veitch Memorial Medal in 1953.

Below, left: The 1898 nursery catalogue of Richard Smith & Co. of Worcester incorporated a posy of flowers and a garden scene.

Below, right: A 1927 nursery catalogue of W. Atlee Burpee, advertising their 'new sweet peas'.

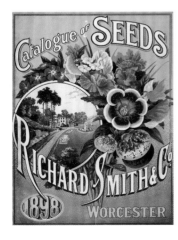

Left: Several apple selections from Hugh Ronald's 1831 *Pyrus Malus Brentfordiensis*, illustrated by Elizabeth Ronalds (*fl.*1830s).

Below left: Hand-coloured printed lithograph entitled *China Aster* by Charles Joseph Hullmandel (1789–1850). Bartholomew's *A Selection of Flowers Adapted Principally for Students* (1821–2) included thirty-six hand-coloured lithographs. It was one of the first works to employ lithography for botanical illustration.

Below right: A watercolour of the auricula primula 'Cockup's Eclipse' (*c.*1810).

Right, top: A librarian replaces books back on the shelves in the Wisley Research Library.

Right, bottom: Regular exhibitions held in the Lindley Library are a chance to view the treasures in the archives and learn more about the world of plants. There are some wonderful paintings and historic posters of Chelsea Flower Show above the bookcases.

'A collection of garden guides documents the changing face of individual gardens, and the collection of over 5,000 postcards of municipal parks is one of only two that are publicly accessible.'

use in design and publications, and to support researchers. However, a programme of strategic digitisation is now underway, with the aim of putting images online for free use by anyone – for non-commercial, educational purposes. At present, the RHS website features an online searchable catalogue, which covers published books and periodicals, and a few items (like the account book of Lancelot 'Capability' Brown and some of Hooker's fruit drawings) are already available to view. The RHS hopes to develop a much richer online platform giving access to catalogue entries for botanical art, photography, archives, ephemera and artefacts – with digital images of selected material. Over time, this resource will grow to enable researchers and gardeners worldwide to explore these internationally important and fascinating collections.

The Lindley Library was refurbished in 2016, one of the first projects in the RHS's ten-year investment programme to be completed, incorporating research rooms and a new exhibition space. Exhibitions in 2018 included 'Healing Garden', about the hidden medicinal history of popular ornamental garden plants as revealed by sixteenth- and seventeenth-century herbals. Public access to the collections has also increased through lectures and courses, among them a six-week introduction to garden history and study days on old book binding and historic glasshouses.

The contents of the RHS libraries will continue to be curated in innovative ways, preserved for future generations and shared as widely as possible. The task of researching and cataloguing this vast collection is ongoing and the library team uncovers new material and new stories all the time. RHS members and members of the British gardening public also generously donate material to help the library record this country's rich gardening heritage. We await news of the latest gems.

# Teabags and bumblebees

### CITIZEN SCIENCE

Anyone can be a citizen scientist. Take Blooms for Bees, a project led by Coventry University to promote and improve gardening for bumblebees. It's simple. You observe, photograph and identify bumblebees (there is a guide to the UK's twenty-four species on the Blooms for Bees website), then submit your data using an app. The information collected will fill gaps in our knowledge about the garden flowers bumblebees prefer to visit, so that gardeners can do more to support these important pollinators. The RHS is one of the project partners, along with the Bumblebee Conservation Trust and Garden Organic.

The RHS has in fact been doing 'citizen science' since long before the term was coined. Historically, the society has collected data through the enquiries that members send to its Advisory Service (see pages 98–101). Appeals in *The Garden* magazine and its forerunners have on occasion asked readers to send in information about pests and diseases. RHS entomologist Andrew Halstead carried out a lily beetle survey in this way in 1990, and there are earlier examples. The arrival of the internet and social media, however, has opened up the possibility to involve many more people and collect data about the natural world on a larger scale.

The first internet-based citizen science survey run by the RHS was launched in 2008 and focused on monitoring the spread of invasive garden insects. Members of the public were asked to fill in an online form to record sightings of four easily recognisable non-native pests: lily beetle, rosemary beetle, hemerocallis gall midge and berberis sawfly; box tree caterpillar was added in 2015. Across the five surveys

more than 47,000 reports were received by the end of 2017, and the effort continues.

Using citizen science in this proactive way helps the RHS to better assess threats and provide accurate advice to gardeners. Datasets are also shared (through the National Biodiversity Network Atlas, for example), to assist further research projects and facilitate collaborations. Not least, this is an excellent way of engaging with members of the public, who, by participating, become part of the worldwide scientific community.

Following on from the web-surveys project, the uses of citizen science have multiplied at the RHS. There was a Honey Fungus Hunt (the data is currently being analysed) and a Rocket Science project involving thousands of schoolchildren (see page 59). RHS and University of Reading PhD student Sarah Duddigan made extensive use of citizen science for her research into how gardeners can best manage their soils. She had help from gardeners all over the UK, who buried teabags in their gardens for three months and then sent them back for analysis in order to better understand the decomposition rates of organic matter. Another PhD project on the diversity of slugs and snails found in UK gardens will be calling on citizen scientists to take part, and all the latest opportunities are signposted on the RHS website. Want to get involved? Who wouldn't?

# RHS website

As a trusted source of news, advice and inspiration for gardeners of all levels of experience, rhs.org.uk contains around 25,000 pages and is Britain's biggest gardening website. It has around 20 million users annually and is a window to the world for every RHS activity, including shows, gardens, events, scientific research, community campaigns and publications. Essential gardening information is available here for everyone, for free, from beginners to experienced gardeners, and on all kinds of subjects, from growing your own fruit and vegetables to rooting cuttings, community gardening and RHS horticultural qualifications. With access to approximately 1,200 advice profiles written by experts, there is no better place to find the latest information on almost any aspect of gardening you can think of.

What makes rhs.org.uk special is the quality and scope of its information. Its gardening advice and science content are underpinned, where possible, by independent scientific research, which is aimed at home gardeners rather than professionals. So if you are wondering how to banish slugs and snails from your garden, or how to bring in the bees and butterflies, the website has a wealth of high-quality information tailored for everyday situations.

Updated every week by a team of editors, the website is constantly evolving. The editorial team collaborates with a large technical team to make sure pages meet the users' needs and expectations, contain the correct type of content, and look fresh and modern. The main website migrated to a new version in 2013–14 and it went mobile responsive in February 2016. With around two-thirds of all website visits being from a mobile device (smartphone or tablet), this means that the website works, and looks great, on any device. Hubs are regularly reviewed, redeveloped and redesigned to make them more user-friendly and easier to navigate.

The website's hugely successful podcasts attract millions of listeners every year. The 'free-to-air' award-winning fortnightly *RHS Gardening Podcast* covers a huge range of horticultural content, from exclusive behind-the-scenes features at RHS flower shows to expert discussions of listeners' gardening queries. In September 2018 a new monthly podcast from *The Garden* magazine was launched, presented by editor Chris Young, who digs a little deeper into the content behind the upcoming issue and interviews people from the world of horticulture.

Fifty years ago, instructions on pruning wisteria would have been described in 1,000 words accompanied by a technical diagram. Now, winter and summer pruning are clearly covered in about two minutes on video. One of the major strengths of the RHS website, which is highly ranked in Google, is its comprehensive and reliable information. No wonder it's trusted and used by millions of people all over the world.

# A connected society

Who would have thought that one day the mother of former One Direction band member Harry Styles would be retweeting an RHS post to her global following of around 2 million. (When the band split in 2015, herbarium staff posted a series of tweets including a clematis with hairy styles . . . ) Analytics revealed it hit a massive audience of teenagers, who then visited the RHS website for the first time. This is just one example of how social media is proving to be an exciting, effective and rapidly evolving way for the RHS to reach out to gardeners of all ages and levels of experience.

Facebook, Twitter, Pinterest and Instagram all busily relay interactions between the society and its followers. The most active channel is Twitter, which very much represents a customer service. Visitors to RHS gardens often use Twitter to post pictures of plants they have seen, asking for identification, and there is a high level of traffic during the RHS show season. Content includes jobs to do in the garden, practical advice linked to the RHS website, and highlights from *The Garden* magazine. Posts also comment on subjects that are trending (such as #beastfromtheeast in February 2018), allowing the RHS to connect with new audiences.

Users interact differently on each platform. On Facebook, they are highly engaged and responsive, providing the greatest number of 'likes'. RHS video- and show-related topics rank among the best performing content on this channel. While the Facebook audience is largely female, aged 50–65, Twitter has a broader demographic. Its followers are more likely to use botanical Latin than those on other platforms, suggesting a certain level of expertise. Whatever the platform, though, RHS content consistently seeks to include people with entry-level knowledge.

Pinterest, where pictures are collected and pinned to a virtual corkboard (and whose core subjects are plants, DIY and baking) is hugely successful for the RHS. Most of the audience are millennials, who generally prefer plants and garden style to practical information. In search of inspiration, their encounters with the RHS on Pinterest can lead them to explore what else the society has to offer.

Instagram, currently the fastest-growing social media channel for the RHS, provides an invaluable link to a younger audience. It is a versatile way for the RHS to get its message across, offering videos, Instagram Stories and newsfeed. Visually led and ideal for sharing high-quality photographs of gardens and flowers, this is a way for the RHS to inspire everyone to grow. Content is constantly being analysed and adjusted: pictures of plants were found to receive a more positive response than those with both plants and people. A portrait of winter twigs (originally published in *The Garden*) received around 3,900 likes, well over double the average response. If trends continue, Instagram will become the main social media platform used by the RHS in the future.

# Publishing across platforms

## PRINT AND DIGITAL

The society has been sharing knowledge in various forms since the first volume of its *Transactions* appeared in 1807. Who knows what Sir Joseph Banks and the other founding fathers would think of the modern media landscape, and the way it continually adapts to changing technology and the needs of different audiences. Today, all that the RHS publishes is overseen by the editorial office in Peterborough. This is where content for magazines, show guides, the website, podcasts, books, internal publishing, and more is commissioned and honed.

The high-quality magazine *The Garden* goes out to all RHS members and is an important channel of communication. It has two main aims: to give members the latest news from across the society; and to reflect wider developments in the horticultural world. A balance of both ensures that members are kept fully up to date. Articles on nursery visits, science and garden design sit beside others on pests and diseases, urban plantings and environmental sustainability. Bespoke images often accompany the text – those showing a comparative collection of cultivars (known as 'plant plates') are always well received.

It is essential that the magazine is trusted by its readership. All images are taken in the correct season and text is read up to eight times before publication. Plant names are checked by taxonomists and scientific references verified by the science team to ensure accuracy. Each issue is planned a year ahead – up to eighteen months for articles like plant profiles.

The RHS also publishes two specialist quarterly, subscription-based publications. *The Plantsman* offers science, nomenclatural updates and in-depth studies on a wide range of plants. *The Orchid Review*, over a century old, became the orchid journal of the RHS in 1993. Covering a range of orchid-related subjects from cultural advice to new plant descriptions and articles on orchid history, it harks back to the great days of 'orchidmania' and the work of botanist John Lindley (1799–1865), who served the society for many years.

The spectrum of RHS publishing is extremely broad. Take the flower shows – each show needs a guide, and these are produced closely with both the website and shows teams. Garden guides – which help visitors get the best from visiting an RHS garden – link to content on the website, and are updated every few years. The *Annual Review and Report*, corporate documents, one-off titles, plant yearbooks and much more are also seen through to publication by the editorial team.

As a book publisher, the RHS has more than 150 titles under its belt. It would be fair to say that it has built a reputation for its more encyclopedic and solutions-based books, many produced since joining forces with Dorling Kindersley in 1987. The best-selling *RHS Encyclopedia of Plants and Flowers* (now in its fifth edition) is a classic example, found on so many gardeners' bookshelves. There are RHS books on fruit and vegetables (*RHS Grow Your Own Veg* by Carol Klein was a big hit), also inspirational and practical titles, but recently there has been an interesting move towards gift publishing (such as *Gardening for Mindfulness* and *Latin for Gardeners*) and this is set to develop.

In line with its work towards maintaining stability in the naming of cultivated plants (see pages 116–19), the RHS continues to publish the *RHS Plant Finder*, registers and supplements (like *The International Dianthus Register* of 2016) and *Sander's List of Orchid Hybrids*, which appears every three years and lists all accepted hybrid genera

**THE ROYAL HORTICULTURAL SOCIETY**

ENCYCLOPEDIA OF
# PLANTS & FLOWERS

EDITOR-IN-CHIEF CHRISTOPHER BRICKELL

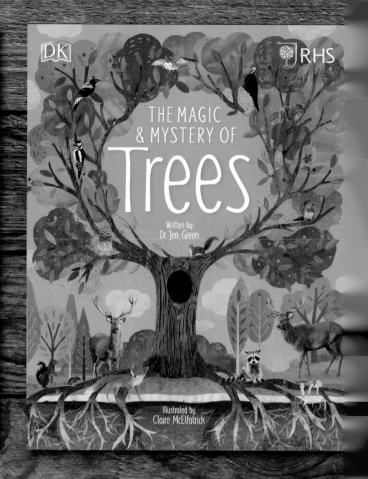

THE MAGIC
& MYSTERY OF
# Trees

Written by
Dr Jen Green

Illustrated by
Claire McElfatrick

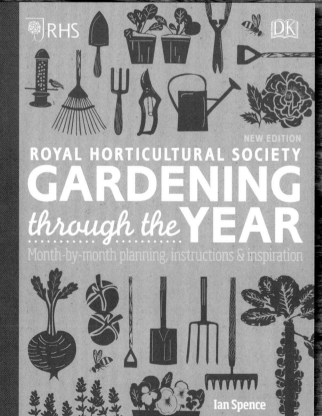

NEW EDITION

**ROYAL HORTICULTURAL SOCIETY**
# GARDENING
## through the YEAR

Month-by-month planning, instructions & inspiration

Ian Spence

A - Z ENCYCLOPEDIA OF
# GARDEN PLANTS

Over 15,000 beautiful plants • The definitive gardener's reference

Sharing the best in Gardening

EDITOR-IN-CHIEF
CHRISTOPHER BRICKELL

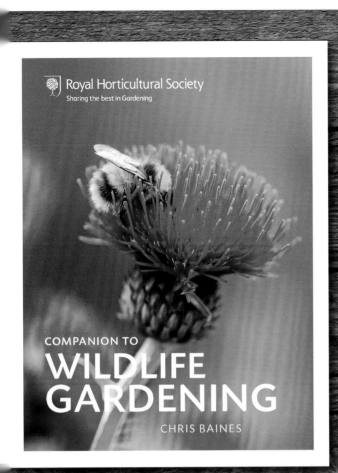

currently in use. Recently, the RHS has returned more fully to its historic role as a specialist publisher, with the *Hillier Manual of Trees and Shrubs*, a series of *Grower Guides* (based on RHS plant trials) and, perhaps most excitingly, some hefty monographs. Authoritative guides to the identification, botany and cultivation of *Kniphofia* (2016), *Hedera* (2017) and *Wisteria* (2019) will be followed by *Colchicum*, *Lathyrus* and *Digitalis*. The RHS is itself a vast storehouse of expertise and its library holds a rich historical archive; with volumes of content so readily available, there is massive potential for specialist titles in the future.

Work published online (rhs.org.uk) is as important these days as printed material; some would say more important, for the RHS gives away – as part of its chartable purpose to inform as many people as possible, all over the world – plenty of hugely valuable content (see page 214). There are two retail websites, for books, gifts and plants, and another dedicated to the Campaign for School Gardening (see pages 58–61). This is a superb resource for anyone wanting to bring the power of plants to Britain's youngsters.

The RHS began publishing podcasts, like little radio shows, a few years ago. The popular fortnightly *RHS Gardening Podcast* updates listeners with news and advice from around the RHS and the horticultural world. The monthly *The Garden Podcast* provides insights into the content of the magazine. Future audio projects – such as oral histories – are being explored in conjunction with the Lindley Library.

Content can be shared so easily nowadays. The RHS has an incredibly active social media department, regularly posting on Facebook, Twitter, Pinterest, Instagram and of course YouTube, so hundreds of thousands of people are sharing in the social world of plants and gardening (see page 215). By including members and non-members through the website, and through social media and podcasts, the RHS has cleverly opened up its reach and influence.

It is a challenge for any organisation to control what it is saying, especially when funds and time are limited, but by expanding its publishing remit, while staying true to the core values of the magazine and books, there is genuine excitement around what is being shared from Britain's leading gardening charity.

Top, left: Currently in its fifth edition, *The RHS Encyclopedia of Plants & Flowers* is an expert guide to choosing the plants for your dream garden, with over 8,000 easy-to-find plants and thousands of photographs.

Top, centre: The RHS is constantly producing new books of all kinds. This publication, aiming to inspire children and filled with fascinating facts about trees, was published in March 2019.

Top, right: Experts on specific areas of horticulture are commissioned to write books on their specialist subjects.

Bottom, left: This practical book takes you through the year, with each chapter looking in-depth at what to do each month.

Bottom, centre: The fully updated fourth edition of this inspirational book contains information on more than 15,000 beautiful plants.

Bottom, right: Adult colouring books have become very popular among those seeking a sense of calm through 'mindfulness' – this book contains forty-five beautiful floral images from the Lindley Library.

AFFILIATED WITH THE ROYAL HORTICULTURAL SOCIETY

Royal Horticultural Society

# Strength in numbers

## AFFILIATED SOCIETIES

Nearly 3,000 local groups are affiliated to the RHS, forming Britain's largest network of gardening clubs and horticultural societies. It is a thriving and lively branch of the society, and one with a surprisingly long history, as revealed by the society's historian, Brent Elliott. It was Sir Charles Wentworth Dilke (1810–69), co-founder of the *Gardeners' Chronicle*, who in 1858 suggested creating a 'union' between the Horticultural Society of London and various provincial horticultural societies. The response was lukewarm at first, even after the proposal was published in the society's journal in 1865. A total of fifty-two societies had signed up to the scheme by 1877, at which point the RHS Council came up with a new idea. They agreed to provide affiliated horticultural and floral societies with RHS medals for distribution at their local exhibitions. The subscription fee was then 5 guineas, which was a substantial sum of money and meant that only wealthy societies could afford to affiliate. (Thankfully, attitudes have changed, and the fees for 2019 are a very reasonable £35.) Some horticultural societies from the 1800s are still thriving. They say the secret is a varied social programme, a strong and active committee, and a willingness to try something new.

The Affiliated Societies Medal was struck in 1901, followed a few years later by the Affiliated Societies Cup. (Today's awards have different names, as you will discover.) In 1908 the first Affiliated Societies Conference was held and by 1916 a lecture programme had expanded to include an RHS panel of 2,000 speakers 'to stimulate the increased production of vegetable food rendered necessary by the war'. Most of Britain's gardening clubs in fact started during the

First or Second World War as part of government initiatives to get us growing our own food.

Today, any gardening club, allotment or horticultural society that holds regular meetings or an annual show, and is involved in promoting horticulture at a local level, is eligible to join. This includes many specialist societies, such as the Orchid Society of Great Britain or the Wakefield and North of England Tulip Society (which has been showing English florists' tulips since 1836). Affiliated groups can be found throughout the UK, and currently range from the Shetland Horticultural Society in the north via the Bakewell & District Organic Gardeners in Derbyshire through to the Jersey Gardening Club in the south. There are even affiliated societies as far away as Argentina and Australia. (For a fascinating story about a gardening club in Germany during the First World War, turn to page 209.)

The scheme helps groups contribute to the local gardening community and encourage more people into gardening. Affiliated societies have access to support and resources, including the RHS list of judges and speakers, gardening advice, tips on how to welcome new members or organise a horticultural show, and editions of both *The Garden* and *Grass Roots* magazines. A free annual outing to one of the RHS gardens (for up to fifty-five members) is one of the most highly prized benefits.

Any affiliated society that holds an annual show can apply for an engraved Banksian Medal (named after the great Joseph Banks, founder member of the RHS), which is awarded to the competitor gaining the highest total number of points across the different horticultural classes (fruit, vegetables and flowers) and is seen as a mark of all-round

221

talent. The Grenfell Medal (named after Francis Grenfell, RHS president 1913–19) is the equivalent honour for floral arrangements.

Local horticultural shows are sometimes seen as the quaint leftover of a bygone age. In fact, they have never been more relevant. Aside from the fun they add to the gardening activities of many people, and the connection with the past they keep alive, they are a wonderful way to bring the community together in a spirit of friendly competition. There are usually show classes for children, schools and adults, so that everyone, whatever their level of experience, can take part. The excitement starts early in the morning on the first day of the show, when people arrive with boxes, vases and sometimes wheelbarrows full of produce, ready to stage their exhibits. Old hands will have their runner beans carefully wrapped in damp cloth or newspaper and their gooseberries in egg boxes filled with cotton wool. Later in the day, judges arrive to marvel over the entries and make the difficult decisions about prizes.

Many clubs are now facing similar challenges and can benefit from pooling their experience, as shown by a forum held in 2018 at RHS Garden Wisley, 110 years after the first Affiliated Societies Conference. The response was overwhelming: all 120 places were reserved in less than ten hours. Society members from different areas met and busily exchanged ideas on how to keep clubs going in the twenty-first century, in particular the need to attract younger members. Embracing social media can help, as can setting up a website and updating it monthly. Some groups are opting for friendlier, more informal names, along the lines of Love2Grow or the Green Fingers Gardening Club. Following on from the successful first event, regular forums will be held at different gardens around Britain, as a way to further unite and strengthen affiliated groups.

While some of the older clubs are struggling due to a lack of members or incoming leaders, new style groups are forming in urban areas. These often focus on horticulture in the community, growing together and involving children, and are less structured. They are less likely to have annual shows, but more likely to support community projects. Whatever form the group takes, what matters is bringing people together through a shared passion for gardening.

Left, top: Plants and gardeners burst into life early in the year in the far south-west, where the RHS-affiliated Cornwall Garden Society holds its Spring Garden Show at Boconnoc.

Left, bottom: The Cottage Garden Society is always welcome in the National Plant Societies' Plant Heritage Marquee at RHS garden shows.

Below: At the Wakefield and North of England Tulip Society annual show, tulips are traditionally displayed in beer bottles.

# Giving and receiving

## PARTNER GARDENS

In a neat link with the past, like meeting up with an old friend, the Hanbury Botanical Gardens at La Mortola, in the Italian Riviera, has recently become an RHS Partner Garden. It is named after the English family that developed it over the course of a century from 1867, using the south-facing slope to grow an extraordinary collection of citrus fruits, palms and other exotics. The moving force behind the garden was none other than Sir Thomas Hanbury. He bought the property as a young man, utterly charmed by the landscape and climate. Later in life, he did something even more remarkable: he donated Wisley to the RHS. The rest, as they say, is history.

The RHS Partner Garden network comprises more than 200 independent gardens across the UK and overseas that generously offer free entry to RHS members at certain times of year. This generosity adds to the appeal of RHS membership and is one of the top reasons for joining the society. As a whole, the scheme aims to inspire visitors through the high standards of design, planting and horticulture shown by each partner garden. Many are well-known, others less so, and there is a mix of styles to interest visitors throughout the year, from formal landscapes to lush woodlands and architectural planting. All do great work in sustaining beautiful gardens for others to enjoy.

The list of partner gardens contains many of the finest gardens in the UK and also a number of unusual ones, such as Godshill Model Village on the Isle of Wight (with bonsai conifers for trees). Then there are the small, privately owned gardens, like Stillingfleet Lodge, near York, and Docton Mill in Devon, where you can often find the owner among the flower beds and have a chat. Fullers Mill Garden, which lies on the banks of the River Lark, in Suffolk, and is owned by the gardening charity Perennial, was one of fourteen gardens to join the scheme in 2018. One day the RHS would like to have a partner garden within easy reach of everyone in the UK.

More than twenty overseas gardens participate, including the famous Arboretum Kalmthout in Belgium. The great gardens of France are well represented, and there is also a partner garden in the Caribbean, the Andromeda Botanic Gardens. Created in Barbados as a family garden by the late Iris Bannochie (1914–88), a recipient of the society's Veitch Memorial Medal, it features tropical gingers and a glorious jade vine (*Strongylodon macrobotrys*) with attendant hummingbirds.

Each garden is expected to meet certain criteria and, in the UK at least, undergoes an assessment before becoming a partner. It needs to be at least 0.8 hectares/2 acres in size, for example, so that it can accommodate groups without overcrowding, and to have the necessary infrastructure. (Extras such as a tea shop or restaurant are always an advantage.) Many garden owners say that being accepted into the scheme is a source of pride, reflecting their hard work and the quality of their garden. Like the RHS, they care passionately about their plant collections and horticultural standards. They also often have their own educational and community programmes. In April 2018, the RHS Community Outreach team joined with Cambo Gardens, near St Andrews, to offer Scottish partner gardens a training day centred around ideas for family and schools activities.

The connection between partner gardens and the RHS enriches

both parties. It could be described as a symbiotic relationship, typical of horticulture. Partner gardens have access to the RHS Advisory Service and can apply for seeds through the RHS Gardens Exchange Scheme. Meetings for partner gardens are held every year, allowing members of the scheme to exchange ideas with each other; and there are horticulturally themed Gardeners' Networking Days at RHS gardens, where participants can meet with the curatorial team. Some of the gardens are very enthusiastic about the partnership; they keep in regular touch about what they are doing and contribute ideas towards the scheme's development. A large proportion have been kindly taking part for more than a decade, including Cawdor Castle in Scotland, Borde Hill in West Sussex, Waterperry in Oxfordshire, Bide-a-Wee Cottage near Newcastle, and Picton Castle in Wales.

Partner gardens can also get involved in plant trials, giving the RHS a way of testing plants in environments different to the Trials Field at Wisley, while giving the partner gardens an area of added interest for their visitors. Floors Castle in Scotland is currently running a daylily (*Hemerocallis*) trial in its walled garden and Abbotsbury in Dorset is assessing hydrangeas. Garden owners and head gardeners represent a fund of knowledge, some of whom lend their expertise as volunteers to the RHS specialist plant committees. Parham Park contributes in this way to the Herbaceous Plant Committee, as does Mount Stewart to the Bulb Committee (see page 122).

Anyone undertaking a tour of the UK in twenty partner gardens would have a hard time making a shortlist. The names alone are often so enticing. How about starting off at the Ascog Hall Fernery

on the Isle of Bute, which is no less than a gardener's paradise. Moving over to the north-west, Holehird, near Windermere, offers beautiful herbaceous borders within a walled garden, a National Collection of Himalayan blue poppies (*Meconopsis*) and views out to the surrounding fells. Inspiration is found at every turn at the Beth Chatto Gardens, in Essex, with its world-famous gravel garden where the planting perfectly matches the growing conditions. In a complete contrast of style, Belvoir Castle, in Leicestershire, is set in pleasure gardens, including a formal rose garden, which give way to a 'Capability' Brown landscape park. This particular tour might end up in the Great Glasshouse at the National Botanic Garden of Wales – but of course, yours could be very different.

Left: Arboretum Kalmthout in Belgium is an inspiring place for tree lovers.

Above: Andromeda Botanic Gardens, Barbados is richly planted with palms and exotic flora.

Right: Belvoir Castle, perched on top of a hill in a 'Capability' Brown landscape, also boasts an attractive rose garden.

Below: The Hydrangea Walk at Abbotsbury Subtropical Garden: a partner garden which took part in the RHS hydrangea trials.

# Green fingers

## SCHOOL OF HORTICULTURE

Every September, around thirty lucky students and fourteen apprentices start an adventure at one of the RHS gardens, where work-based training allows them to turn classroom theory into real-life practice. The society has been training gardeners for more than a century, offering them a springboard towards an exciting future. Over 550,000 people are employed as a result of ornamental horticulture in the UK, so fresh training is constantly required to ensure the industry is supplied with the skills it needs.

The School of Horticulture was established at RHS Garden Wisley in 1907, where it originally occupied rooms in the Laboratory. Among the requirements of the Wisley Diploma in Practical Horticulture was a collection of at least 200 dried specimens of the local flora, properly named, mounted and labelled. Students, who were unpaid, lodged in nearby towns and villages and were encouraged to arrive at 6 a.m. each day for 'undirected observation' before starting work.

New student accommodation, Aberconway House, was opened in 1952 by Sir David Bowes-Lyon, who pronounced: 'I hope we may look forward to the steady emergence of a whole string of Joseph Paxtons.' Wisley's students are still housed in shared accommodation, in Wisley village, and the pursuit of high standards continues across all RHS gardens. Those who are awarded the prestigious RHS Apprenticeships and Diplomas in Horticultural Practice are expected to maintain the reputation for excellence set by the RHS throughout their career.

Many RHS students and apprentices go on to work in and lead public, historic or private gardens. RHS students are also nursery owners, educators, authors, journalists, landscape and garden designers, arborists, show managers and consultants. Wisley's curator Matthew Pottage, celebrated garden designer Dan Pearson and Mike Nelhams, head gardener of Tresco Abbey Gardens, are all alumni of the RHS School of Horticulture.

Since 2015, the society's gardens have delivered bespoke RHS training programmes which are recognised within the regulated qualifications framework. The Level 3 Diploma in Horticultural Practice has been offered at RHS gardens Harlow Carr, Rosemoor and Hyde Hall as a one-year course. The Level 4 Diploma in Horticultural Practice is a two-year course based at Wisley, where students cover Level 3 in their first year. Both qualifications remain highly respected in the industry. Applicants need to have a Level 2 qualification and some work experience in horticulture to apply. Equally important is enthusiasm, commitment and a dedication to succeed.

Some applicants have had horticulture as their vocation from an early age, while others have chosen to make it their second (or even third) career. Each year there are around 250 applicants for 36 places, and usually there is a roughly equal male–female split, which is welcome news as the School of Horticulture did not start to accept female candidates until the 1970s.

Students work alongside RHS horticulturists across the gardens' departments, gaining experience in caring for ornamental and edible plants. Around a third of their working time is devoted to lectures, trips to historic gardens and local growers, skills masterclasses (including basic soil cultivation and bamboo management), visits to RHS shows and (in Level 4) specialist plant committee meetings. Students say that it is hard work, but extremely valuable.

Above: Students learn to cultivate, prune and harvest; vertical cordons of redcurrants make picking easy.

Left: Thinning bunches of grapes is an art that requires skill, patience and dexterity.

Right: There is a correct way to make a climbing-bean wigwam; students learn from Wisley staff, who have years of practical gardening experience.

'The society has been training gardeners for more than a century, offering them a springboard towards an exciting future.'

The Level 3 course looks at how to manage plants in different locations, to control weeds, prune, and select the 'right plant for the right place'. Students are kept up to date on issues in plant health to safeguard the future of the industry. They gain an understanding of horticultural taxonomy and plantsmanship, so the collections they oversee throughout their careers will be correctly named. Level 4 builds on this knowledge, and additional modules on garden design cover the importance of horticulture for health, wellbeing and the environment. Students look at invasive alien species, the future of herbaria, the vital role of seed banks, and other current issues. The challenges set are considerable, but the rewards for achievement are high.

For those new to horticulture, a two-year apprenticeship programme aimed primarily (but not exclusively) at 16- to 19-year-olds is available in all RHS gardens. Apprentices work in the gardens' departments and help RHS staff with day-to-day tasks. This is complemented by day or block release to college, adding a national apprenticeship qualification to their RHS-endorsed work experience. The aim is for apprentices to increase their skills, confidence and knowledge and find successful, satisfying employment within horticulture as a result. New for 2019 is an arboriculture and machinery apprenticeship at RHS Garden Bridgewater.

There are also opportunities for a one-year specialist placement at Wisley, within the Glasshouse, Fruit and Vegetable, Rock and Alpine or Arboriculture teams. Primarily a practical experience, it also includes CV-enhancing academic work to increase the student's potential for future employment.

The School of Horticulture fits within the wider educational provision of the RHS, an awarding-winning organisation regulating eleven qualifications delivered in 100 approved centres in the UK and around the world, as well as by distance learning. Over 5,000 individuals a year gain an RHS qualification at Levels 1, 2 and 3. The most prestigious qualification is the RHS Master of Horticulture, a degree-level programme delivered by blended learning, which is aimed at horticultural professionals who have been in the industry for over four years.

Of course, to get people to the level of professional qualifications, it is important that they have the chance to discover horticulture in the first place. The RHS provides opportunities for 45,000 young people to visit its gardens and take part in learning sessions each year, in addition to running informal courses and workshops for adults, from beginner gardeners to professionals. The RHS Campaign for School Gardening provides support to inspire children within schools (see pages 58–61). On all these fronts, the RHS is making a difference to people's lives.

Left: Florence Mansbridge received a bursary to study the rich and varied flora of South Africa's Western Cape.

Right: Ben Ram undertook a 'Study of the High Altitude *Proteaceae* in the Western Cape of South Africa', studying their habitat and growing conditions and collecting seed.

# A world of opportunities

## BURSARIES

Over 100 grants are awarded annually by the RHS for study tours, expeditions, voluntary work at botanic or historic gardens, research, botanical art and other projects with a clear relevance to horticulture. The destination may be somewhere in Britain or a country on the other side of the world. RHS bursaries have recently taken people to Tasmania, Japan, Mexico, China, Costa Rica, the United States and Canada.

This is a scheme that the RHS holds dear, as a way to support continuing professional development and to raise the status of horticulture within the British economy. Anyone involved in horticulture, or related disciplines, can apply, including professional and student gardeners, career changers, botanists, soil scientists and even knowledgeable amateur gardeners. Applications are put before the RHS Bursaries Committee, a group of independent horticultural experts from a wide range of fields. A total of over £150,000 is awarded every year and individual grants range from £100 to £3,000.

Funding for RHS bursaries is provided through endowments and donations from members of the public whose wish is to add to the sum of knowledge within the world of horticulture. Sometimes donors request to support specific areas, and the Bursaries Committee ensures that this is respected. To increase the impact of each bursary award, recipients are asked to share the knowledge gained in as many ways as possible, through social media, presentations and articles, and also in person to encourage other potential applicants. Florence Mansbridge, senior horticulturist at the Eden Project in Cornwall, said of her time getting to know the flora of South Africa's Western

Cape: 'I have learnt so much from this trip. You really can't beat going to see plants growing in their native habitats.'

Recipients submit a written report within three months of completing their project, and these become public documents available both online and through the library at RHS Garden Wisley. Two annual bursary report prizes are awarded; one for the highest standard of report-writing and the other to the person judged to have gained the most from their project.

The RHS collaborates with the National Garden Scheme (NGS) to offer the Elspeth Thompson Bursary in support of community gardening projects that bring people together and inspire a love of gardening across all age groups. The projects funded by this bursary are particularly diverse.

The Interchange Fellowship is an Anglo-American exchange programme sponsored jointly by the RHS and The Garden Club of America. It allows British horticultural students and graduates to take up a year-long internship at Longwood Gardens, Pennsylvania, or attend the first year of a horticulture-related postgraduate course in an American university. A reciprocal arrangement is available to American applicants. Founded in 1948, the programme has funded more than 100 fellows, many of whom go on to occupy leading positions in botanic gardens, education and landscape architecture.

The attraction of developing a new
garden at RHS Bridgewater is a
once-in-a-lifetime opportunity.

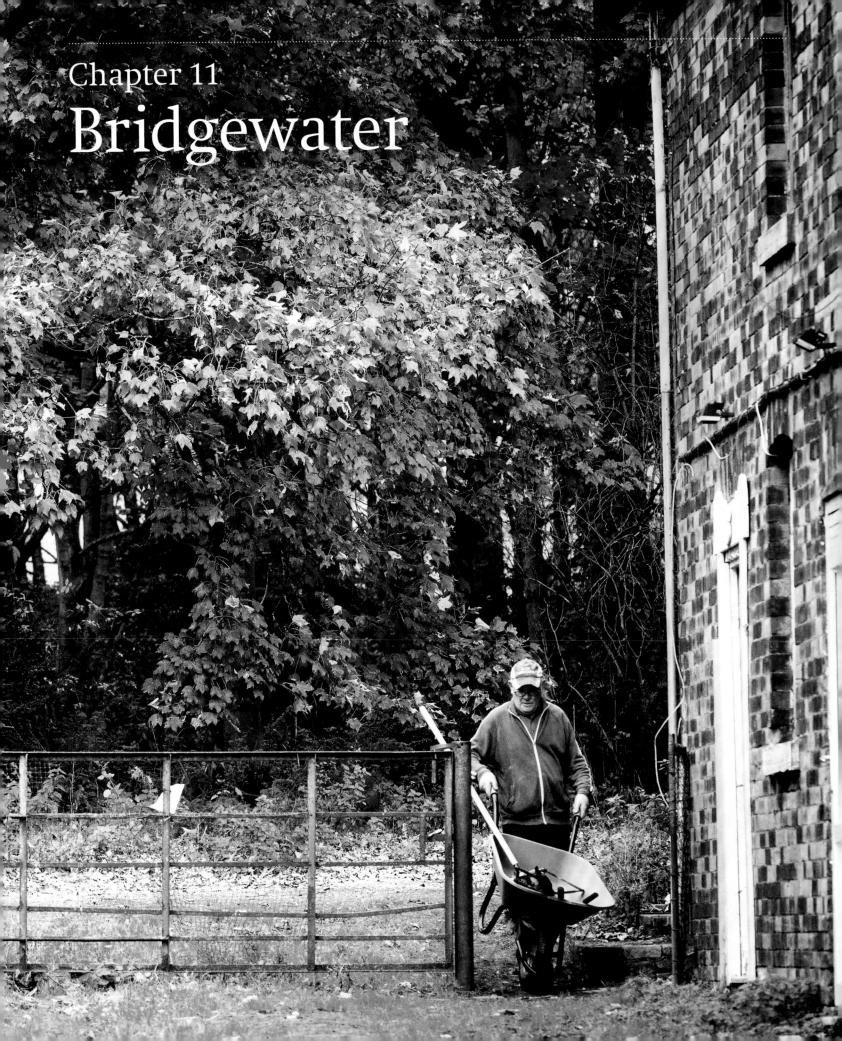

# Chapter 11
# Bridgewater

Left: The Gardener's Cottage is one of the few surviving reminders of the great estate at Worsley, now RHS Garden Bridgewater.

Right: Worsley New Hall as it was in 1927.

# Bridgewater

## GREATER MANCHESTER GARDEN

On 18 April 2017 an advance team of RHS staff moved into an office in the grounds of Worsley New Hall, a derelict historic estate close to the city centres of Salford and Manchester. It was a small occasion in itself and yet represents a landmark in the society's 200-year history: the start of its first urban garden. Unlike the four other RHS gardens, each gifted to the society with existing horticultural strengths and an established palette of plants, this one was searched for and chosen, and will be created almost from scratch. Ideally situated to serve the north-west of Britain, this exciting project is the outcome of a collaboration between Peel Land and Property, Salford City Council and the RHS, resulting in a 999-year lease on the site.

Over the coming years, the 62-hectare/154-acre grounds at Worsley New Hall, once home to the Earls of Ellesmere, will be transformed into a world-class destination called RHS Garden Bridgewater. It is a huge undertaking. The Victorian mansion at the heart of the estate was demolished in 1949, by which time the glorious formal gardens had already slipped into decline. The RHS plans to breathe new life into this lost landscape, which is an important part of Salford's heritage and is valued by local residents. The garden's potential as an asset for the community will be developed jointly with its aspiration for horticultural excellence, and those who have never before planted or pruned will be welcomed as warmly as the keenest of gardeners.

While all that remains of the mansion are two basement floors filled in with rubble, the contours of a huge, formal Victorian terrace have survived and still step down to an ornamental lake. This was carved out in the 1840s and is now partially silted up. To the west are the remains of a pleasure ground, today known as Middlewood, containing venerable trees and some massive original specimens of *Rhododendron* 'Christmas Cheer' and *R.* 'Cynthia'. Beyond this lies a 4.5-hectare/11-acre walled garden, one of the largest in Britain, and the vestiges of an orchard. On the southern edge of the site is a large meadow fringed by the Bridgewater Canal, which opened in 1761 and transported coal from mines at Worsley to industrial areas of Manchester.

In its heyday, the estate twice received Queen Victoria; the canal was even dyed blue in honour of the royal barge. The ornamental plantings of that time have all but disappeared, although a detailed inventory of the wilderness may yet reveal some special trees or shrubs. Hidden within the grounds are several architectural gems, including an ice house, a grotto on an island and a chimney that once served a series of glasshouses. These original features will be lovingly restored, along with some from later periods (a 1950s anti-aircraft bunker, for instance) and will form part of the new garden designed by influential landscape architect Tom Stuart-Smith. His masterplan for Bridgewater shows how visitors will enter at the south, through a new Welcome Building set beside its own lake; this links by streams and cascades to the main lake. Paths will lead visitors into a perennial meadow adjoining the walled garden, then through woods up to the historic terraces.

The masterplan lays out the broad lines of the site's future development, while the creative evolution of the garden will be steered by a group of garden advisers and the RHS's in-house team of horticultural specialists. In the first phase, comprising an ambitious set of targets for completion by the garden's opening in 2020, the magnificent walled garden will become a sequence of distinct spaces, with Tom Stuart-Smith's Paradise Garden occupying the inner section.

Influenced by early Islamic styles, its tranquil pool surrounded by Mediterranean and Asian plants is designed to instil a state of mindfulness. Adjoining this will be a separate Wellbeing Garden, community teaching plots and large Kitchen Garden containing 115 cultivated beds. A horticultural service yard, new glasshouses, orchard and science trials area will also take shape here.

As the garden develops, the RHS is seeking to involve local people and allow space for a sense of ownership to develop. Consequently, construction work is being carried out by local contractors, trainees and apprentices, enthusiastically supported by hundreds of volunteers and nearby community projects, housing associations and social care charities. Once complete, the site will be readily accessible by public transport, and there are plans for a cycle path along the Bridgewater Canal and another connecting with Walkden railway station.

This is the largest hands-on gardening project the RHS has ever tackled. Clearance of the walled garden alone was an enormous task. Heaps of brambles and around 500 trees were removed, mainly self-seeded sycamore and downy birch, but also over-mature nursery trees and bloated Leyland cypress hedging. Any trees with heritage, landscape or ecological value were earmarked for saving before work began, in close consultation with the local arboricultural officer.

The site's precise growing conditions and ecology are gradually being assessed. Soils, which will be protected during construction, or relocated for later use, are varied and suited to a range of plants. The areas of sandy loam and clay offer different opportunities to the peaty soil of the meadows by the canal. What already marks Bridgewater out horticulturally is the favourable climate of the walled garden. Planting will blend the tried-and-tested with fresh ideas to push the boundaries of what can be grown in the region. Some collections from other RHS gardens will also be relocated here, notably Wisley's gooseberries.

One of the first operations for RHS staff in spring 2017 was to safeguard the orchard's twenty-three ancient pear trees. Hard pruning has encouraged the growth of young shoots for scion wood, allowing new specimens to be grafted. The trees have been DNA-tested and all identified except for one, which is unknown to the National Fruit Collection at Brogdale and will hopefully turn out to be a local pear with a fascinating history.

Repairs soon began to the 1.4 kilometres/1530 yards of dilapidated, cracked and leaning red-brick walls surrounding the walled garden. The outer walls are around 1.5 metres/5 feet high and enclose a set of taller inner walls. The tallest, standing at 4.5 metres/15 feet, are found in the centre. Facing an array of different aspects, they are ideal for growing apricots, peaches and figs.

The new kitchen garden will take advantage of this to display ornamentally trained fruit trees in the form of cordons and espaliers. Covering 0.7 hectares/1¾ acres, it will include a permaculture forest, a traditional Victorian potager and a less formal section including ornamental and dye plants, all offering visitors ideas to suit any size of space. The kitchen garden is the outcome of a nationwide competition won by Chelsea Flower Show Gold medallists Charlotte Harris and Hugo Bugg, whose design ingeniously incorporates references to local history. The garden's arterial pathways form a pattern inspired by the underground network of mining canals known as the Worsley Navigable Levels, along which coal was brought to the surface. The borders, on the other hand, are laid out following a nineteenth-century Ordnance Survey map and reflect the agricultural landscape.

Left: An aerial view shows the extent of the work that has been undertaken. The walled garden is centre right; to the left is a new car park.

Above: The project relies heavily on the skills and enthusiasm of volunteers. When people work together, productivity is improved and it is more fun. The work is inclusive; it is a diverse community of enthusiasts with one aim: to help create the new garden.

## The Plant Factory

Two landscape architect students – Stella Yang and Karsan Karavadra from Manchester Metropolitan University – won an RHS competition to design a new Learning Garden, which will be part of the Walled Garden at RHS Bridgewater. Their design, called 'The Plant Factory', based on the idea of plants as machines, will teach all ages about the nature of plants and how they work. It will be modular, so it can be moved to suit different users, and recycled materials are employed wherever possible. Highlights include an 'Eco-Chimney', with bird and bat boxes, a 'Workhouse Greenhouse' for exotic plants and a test area for experiments.

The Wellbeing Garden will provide local groups with opportunities for practical gardening, particularly charities helping people with health and addiction problems. For this area, a process of consultation is ensuring that the design closely fits the needs of the users. Conversations have led to a three-way division of space – social, meditative and active – for community activities, relaxation and horticultural therapy.

The community teaching plots, the fourth section of the walled garden, form a patchwork of different sized borders where local residents can grow crops, ornamentals and structural plants like willow and bamboo for their own use. Access will be targeted to help a wider range of people get involved in gardening, and it is hoped that refugees will be among those who benefit. Four of the plots will be set aside for RHS apprentices, whose mission is to guide novices and gardeners new to growing in the British climate; in doing this, they will embed in their own minds the knowledge passed on by their tutors, creating a ripple effect of learning.

The RHS is working with the University of Salford's Centre for Applied Archaeology to capture memories of the garden's past, eventually to weave into the experience of visiting Bridgewater. After it was sold in 1923, the estate served different purposes. In the Second World War the grounds were used for military training. Later, a garden centre, scout camp and rifle range came and went. Local people have lived, worked or played here over the years, and a deep-running affection for the place is what motivates many volunteers involved in the new garden.

One remarkable story began when demolition work unearthed a jam jar containing a yellowing builder's time sheet from 1964. The Bridgewater team posted the document on social media and within twenty-four hours had located one of the four men named on it: Eddie Dootson, now in his seventies and still living locally, who had worked for a period in the walled garden. A lifelong allotmenteer, he arrived for his first visit back at Bridgewater with a sackful of trophies and a newspaper clipping of *Coronation Street* actress Violet Carson presenting him with an award for his champion dahlias. Eddie got involved with Bridgewater and began growing dahlias again, taking on a member of the RHS community outreach team as apprentice. Their first crop of blooms was displayed in an RHS marquee at a community event on the lawns in front of Salford Civic Centre in 2018.

As it evolves, RHS Garden Bridgewater is capturing the imagination of local partners in unexpected ways. A Manchester group is raising funds for a streamside garden of Chinese plants, and a nearby sugar-art collective has come up with several creative proposals. In an exciting development, the BBC Philharmonic, which is based in Salford, has commissioned Tom Coult to compose a new work in praise of urban nature. The piece will be performed for the first time in 2020 at Manchester's Bridgewater Hall, in celebration of the RHS's fifth garden.

In the years to come, Bridgewater will enter a second phase of development, bringing in an arboretum and a Learning Centre with its own teaching garden. The lost terraces, originally designed by William Andrews Nesfield (1794–1881), will be reworked, and the civil defence bunker converted into an exhibition space. In place of the manor house, on its ledge of high ground, will stand an awe-inspiring glasshouse as the pinnacle of any visit. It is hoped that a Northern College of Horticulture may also be established here in the future. The new RHS garden at Bridgewater has all the makings of a national garden with a local heart.

Opposite, top: An artist's impression of the flower garden inside the Walled Garden at RHS Bridgewater. It is based on the concept of a paradise garden, complete with lily pond.

Opposite, bottom left: Tom Stuart-Smith, creator of the masterplan, and RHS Ambassador for Bridgewater Garden, Carol Klein, discuss the proposed plans.

Opposite, bottom right: The 'engine house' with its impressive chimney stack was built in the early 1840s and designed to accommodate the Rochester boiler, which heated the old walled garden and nearby glasshouses.

Left: As the garden evolves, existing and new planting decisions have to be made.

Above: Clearing trees and shrubs is hard work, but invigorating and ultimately very satisfying. You can see how much has been achieved at the end of each day.

The RHS wants to improve everyone's lives through plants, and fill their lives with flowers.

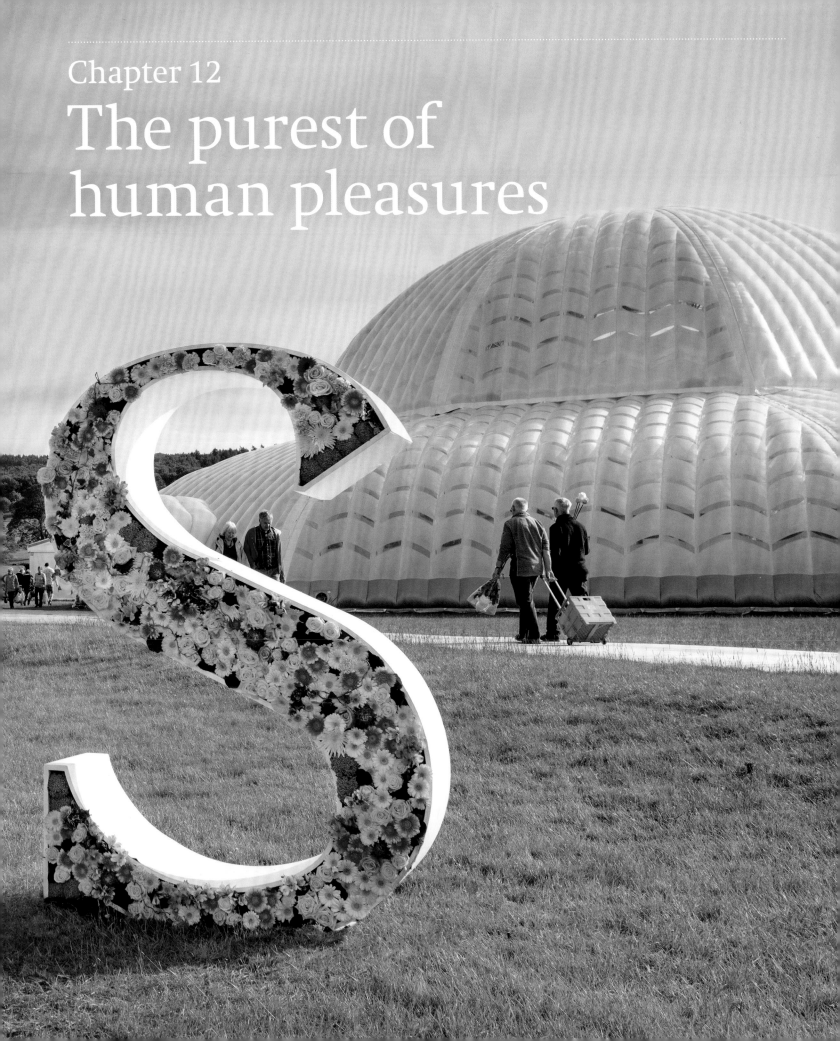

# Chapter 12

# The purest of human pleasures

Left: One of the easiest ways to create a floral area is growing annuals from seed. It brightens up an area, makes you feel good and is beneficial to pollinators.

Right: Director General Sue Biggs has led the transformation of the RHS, making it relevant for the twenty-first century.

# The purest of human pleasures

## THE RHS VISION

When I began writing this book, I went to meet the director general of the RHS, Sue Biggs, to ask exactly what message she wanted to deliver. Her underlying response was: 'I want people to know how the RHS has changed, and how plants can transform people's lives.' The interview finished with the advice that I should attend the next induction course. So I did. From the second the course started, at 10 a.m. on 25 January 2018, in the Garden Hall, Wisley, my perception of the RHS began to change. It was gradual at first but rapidly gained momentum. As the talks unfolded, there followed a process of revelation, information and education. I began jotting down notes and the same thought recurred: 'Why don't people know that?'

As a 'traditional' and long-standing RHS member, what was revealed at that induction was unlike anything I had heard before. Staff detailed their mission 'to inspire passion and excellence in the science, art and practice of horticulture'. Their guiding principles – to inspire, involve, inform, improve – dovetailed with a vision 'to enrich everyone's life through plants, and make the UK a greener and more beautiful place'. Finally, the message was to unleash and increase the power of gardening in everyone.

These are high ideals for such a gentle hobby, and I came to see how they have emerged at a time when the impact of horticulture has been scientifically analysed as never before. Academic research reveals that gardening improves quality of life, mitigates climate change and brings communities together. It crystallised in my mind that horticulture is not just a pleasant pastime but an activity of vital importance to the welfare of the world and its inhabitants, some of

whom may never have considered gardening before. The only charity with the skills and capacity to turn this multifaceted vision into reality and explore its potential was the RHS. It had become their responsibility. If they didn't do it, who would?

A 2012 survey suggested that gardeners and florists were the happiest workers in the UK – but could something as fundamental as horticulture really have such a life-enhancing, even world-changing impact? The answer is yes. Our ancestors were hunter-gatherers who lived in and from the landscape. When they settled down into communities, plants formed their natural habitat and cultivation became part of their occupation. Francis Bacon said in his 1625 essay 'Of Gardens': 'God Almighty first planted a garden and indeed, it is the purest of human pleasures'; and in Arabic, the word for 'garden' also means 'paradise'. It seems that we are genetically predisposed to garden. How fitting, then, that gardens and horticulture should help take us away from the stresses of the alien environment that many live in today.

Gardening has revealed itself to be almost a cure-all. Suffering from mental problems? Garden regularly. Need an antidote to loneliness? Garden in groups. Need physical exercise and a change of diet? Take one allotment and go straight to the (veg) bed. If gardening is a key to the health of the nation, it may also be a key to the health of the world by mitigating the effects of climate change.

This is why the 'new' RHS is working for change. There is now a realisation that the organisation's impact can extend to all parts of society, through community outreach, its gardens and publications, schools, colleges, specialist societies and gardening clubs. But there are still exciting avenues to be explored, which involve adapting to the modern world.

At the last Urban Show at the RHS Lindley and Lawrence Halls in London, in October 2018, I discovered a generation who were passionate about gardening and the environment. They were not the traditional RHS demographic, but vibrant young people, hipsters and millennials, part of what is known as 'generation rent', potentially living long-term in flats, lofts and rented houses. These people are aware of climate change, want to bring the natural world into their artificial environments, and are passionate about plants. Due to their boundless enthusiasm, houseplants are enjoying the kind of resurgence that would thrill the Victorians with their plant-filled homes and conservatories. This generation has found a perfect outlet for their style, sharing images of terraria and horticulturally embellished interiors on social media platforms, particularly Instagram, where influencers have thousands of followers. Shops specialising in houseplants have sprouted up.

If the RHS wants to tap into the current interest in gardening in the younger generations, they must continue to exploit fully the potential of social media. The people I spoke to at the show had heard about it from friends on social media, but were not totally clear about the role of the RHS. This new audience receives information through a device that rarely leaves the hand. The mobile phone provides everything that newspapers and magazines once did. In a time where you can sit on your sofa at home and buy something off the internet just by speaking, the RHS must find a way to attract their attention.

They also need to be spoken to in the way they communicate with each other, and to identify with the person who is delivering the message. It is not with the same tone or content as captivates older, knowledgeable horticulturists. 'Generation rent' needs down-to-earth

'If gardening is a key to the health of the nation, it may also be a key to the health of the world by mitigating the effects of climate change.'

The RHS London Urban Garden Show was attended by a new generation of enthusiasts, whose passion for houseplants is turning our cities into a real urban jungle.

Above: A wildlife-friendly plot can still be manicured and tidy, like this one at Framfield Allotments in Ealing, London.

Left: Visitors just love a walk through a wild-meadow-style garden, especially when it is designed by Piet Oudolf. This design at Hampton Court Palace Flower Show earned him the inaugural RHS Horticultural Hero award in 2018.

Below: Youth Takeover Day at Wisley in 2017 included a Social Media Challenge. Post-it notes played a major part in planning their online campaigns.

Right: A jolly band of gardeners carrying plants from the RHS Hampton Court Palace Flower Show plant adoption scheme. This innovative recycling scheme allows plants from flower shows to be adopted by the public. Thousands of plants have been re-homed.

but effective gardening information delivered in a way that is fun, not over-complicated, and relevant to their needs. Live streams for those who can't get to the flower shows, video content on Instagram stories, and online text with photos have the potential to reach out to an ever-growing audience who use these platforms. They could almost be seen as an unofficial affiliated society. The RHS has a YouTube channel and social media, but often it is older people speaking to older people. We need to hear the voice of more young people. Like the schoolchildren, they are the gardeners of the future.

There are 195 nations in the world, and then there is the nation of gardeners. The gardening nation knows no boundaries – we all dig the same earth. For many people in Britain and across the world, whether displaced by events or choosing to live abroad, gardening is a reminder of home and a link with their past. It is often a source of solace. I once met Mr Afsal, a farmer from Pakistan whom fate had decreed should end up gardening on an allotment in Bradford. His need to till the earth and grow plants never left him.

But what of the RHS future? There are likely to be increased efforts to push international membership, especially in areas with similar climates to that of Britain, where the gardening advice and plants will be equally relevant. Once RHS Garden Bridgewater is established (opening in 2020), there will be an opportunity to develop more RHS links in areas of Britain where there is currently no RHS garden. Continued research into climate change, biosecurity, plant health and human wellbeing should ensure that the society will have greater influence as a political voice in these areas. The Horticulture Matters campaign will become more influential and community outreach will continue to expand. However, change needs to be undertaken with caution. There is the danger that the organisation may go off in too many directions, in an attempt to capitalise on the many benefits of horticulture. While the focus is quite rightly fixed on extending its charitable work, there is the risk of neglecting the core members who visit the gardens and support the society in many other ways. One of the great strengths of the RHS is its history, and the past should be used as the foundation for the future. The RHS still has some way to go in becoming more inclusive, which is a considerable challenge and needs resolving with thought, diplomacy and care. It is capable of achieving this.

There is much to be done and much being done. I was reminded of the RHS while watching bees at work in a glass beehive displayed at the RHS Flower Show Tatton Park in 2018. Everywhere on the honeycomb were bees in organised yet fevered activity, a mass of movement with a thousand things happening at once and they all knew what to do. Not one bee was standing still.

When I began writing this book, I didn't know what the RHS wanted to achieve.

We do now.

Horticulture is at the heart of
everything we do.

# Index

## ACKNOWLEDGMENTS

My thanks to everyone at the RHS who gave their valuable time to be interviewed, especially Sir Nicholas Bacon, Sue Biggs (no relation to me), Alistair Griffiths and Yvette Harvey, Leigh Hunt, Anna da Silva and Gerard Clover.

I am also grateful to Talia Sender-Galloway for the induction course; Rob Brett, Ian Le Gros and Jonathan Webster for their rapid responses; Anna Skibniewski-Ball for going the extra mile; and Gemma Lake for being so willing to answer my questions.

Karen Culpin provided invaluable help, as did members of the RHS specialist plant committees, particularly Dr Nuala Sterling, Mike Pitcher and John Anderson; also Pam Hayward and David Millais of the RHS Rhododendron, Camellia and Magnolia Group; and Orchid Committee members Dr Henry Oakeley, Dr John Elliott and Peter Sander; Jason Ingram contributed many beautiful photographs.

Staff at the Lindley Library and Archives assisted valiantly with research, especially Fiona Davison and Susan Robin. I owe a debt of gratitude likewise to Dr Brent Elliott, author of *The RHS: A History 1804–2004*.

A special mention is reserved for Roy Lancaster and Jacqui Cottam. I would also like to thank Tim Sandall and Jim Buttress for their hilarious but unusable stories; Jess Cook of Silver Ball PR; Lee Connelly, the Skinny Jean Gardener; Lucy Pitman at Plant Heritage; and Hazel and Julie Aylett.

Staff at RHS publications were a great support, particularly Michelle Housden, who replied so rapidly to my requests, Tim Berry, Chris Young and Rae Spencer-Jones. I am grateful to Helen Griffin at White Lion Publishing for asking me to write this book; to Michael Brunström for all the picture research; to Sarah Zadoorian for her total commitment to ensuring that the text was as informative and lively as possible; and also to Simon Maughan.

This book is dedicated to Gill, Jessica, Henry and Chloe Biggs for their continued patience; Bill and Joy Parkin, Jean Baillie, Catherine Purkis, David Hurrion and Debs Stephen for their encouragement; and to the late Khun Vichai for bringing such happiness and success to the people of Leicester.

First published in 2019 by White Lion Publishing
an imprint of The Quarto Group
The Old Brewery, 6 Blundell Street
London N7 9BH
United Kingdom

www.QuartoKnows.com

A catalogue record for this book is available from the British Library.

ISBN  978 0 7112 3935 7
Ebook ISBN  978 0 7112 4179 4

10 9 8 7 6 5 4 3 2 1
2023 2022 2021 2020 2019

Typeset in Swift and FS Albert
Design by Glenn Howard

RHS Publisher: Rae Spencer-Jones
RHS Editor: Simon Maughan
RHS Picture Editor: Julian Weigall
RHS Head of Editorial: Chris Young

Printed in China

Royal Horticultural Society
80 Vincent Square
London SW1P 2PE
Tel: 020 3176 5800
rhs.org.uk
@The_RHS

Brimming with creative inspiration, how-to projects and useful
information to enrich your everyday life, Quarto Knows is a favourite
destination for those pursuing their interests and passions. Visit our
site and dig deeper with our books into your area of interest: Quarto
Creates, Quarto Cooks, Quarto Homes, Quarto Lives, Quarto Drives,
Quarto Explores, Quarto Gifts, or Quarto Kids.